ID0629616

WITHDRAWN

7199

Straight Talk
About Anger

Straight Talk About Anger

Christine Dentemaro and
Rachel Kranz

 Facts On File®

AN INFOBASE HOLDINGS COMPANY

STRAIGHT TALK ABOUT ANGER

Facts On File, Inc.
460 Park Avenue South
New York NY 10016

Library of Congress Cataloging-in-Publication Data
Dentemaro, Christine.
    Straight talk about anger / Christine Dentemaro and Rachel Kranz.
        p. cm.
    Includes bibliographical references and index.
    ISBN 0-8160-3079-0 (alk. paper)
    1. Anger in adolescence. [1. Anger.] I. Kranz, Rachel.
    II. Title.
    BF724.3.A55D46 1995   94-34591
    152.4'7—dc20

Facts On File books are available at special discounts when purchased in bulk quantities for businesses, associations, institutions or sales promotions. Please call our Special Sales Department in New York at 212/683-2244 or 800/322-8755.

Text design by Catherine Rincon Hyman
Jacket design by Dorothy Wachtenheim

Printed in the United States of America

MP FOF 10 9 8 7 6 5 4 3 2 1

This book is printed on acid-free paper.

About the Straight Talk About . . . series:

The Straight Talk About . . . books provide young adult readers with the most factual, up-to-date information available. Recognizing that the teen years are a time of growth and transition, the authors aim not to dispense any easy answers or moral judgments but to help young people clarify a number of issues and difficult choices and to consider the consequences of their decisions. Each book is throughly indexed and contains a directory of resources.

Contents

Special thanks to Gladys Foxe, C.S.W.

1

Anger: The Misunderstood Emotion

Theo* has been boiling all day. First his English teacher told him that she was marking him down a full grade on his composition, just because the margins weren't wide enough. Then his basketball coach made the whole team do extra laps just because one of the guys didn't bring the right practice clothes. At his after-school job at the grocery store, Theo's boss told him that he'd have to work all day Saturday, even though Theo had already made plans to go to the lake with some friends that day. When Theo gets home, he finds that his three-year-old brother has somehow spilled milk all over Theo's desk—and when Theo starts to yell at his brother, his mother comes in and yells at *him*. Dinner is liver and onions, a meal that Theo hates, but in his home, he's

---

*Everyone identified by first name only in this book is a *composite*—a portrait drawn from details that come from many different people.

not allowed to leave the table until he finishes every bite. After dinner, Theo's girlfriend calls and tells him she can't go out with him on Saturday night because her cousin Ronny is visiting from out of town and she'll be spending the evening with him. When it's time to go to bed, Theo can't sleep. He just lies there playing every conversation over again in his head, thinking about what he should have done and said differently to make the day go better.

Everybody knows that Mary Ellen is one of the sweetest girls you'll ever meet. She's always nice and cheerful, always so helpful and willing to get along. When her parents ask her to spend the weekend baby-sitting her younger brothers and sisters, she's happy to stay home and help out. If her boyfriend shows up an hour late for a date without calling, Mary Ellen understands that he was hanging out with his friends and just lost track of the time. If her best friend Lissa calls at the last minute to cancel their trip to the mall because that great guy in their English class just asked her out, Mary Ellen doesn't mind at all—in fact, she's happy for her friend. Mary Ellen's only problem is that sometimes she gets these terrible headaches. Then *she* has to cancel all of her plans, and because the pain is so bad, she just has to go lie down for a while.

Scott and Julia have been going out for a few months now. Usually they get along very well, but sometimes they fight. Julia is the kind of person who gets mad very quickly, says what she thinks, and then it's over. Although she's never unfair or cruel, she does raise her voice, speak emphatically ("I just can't stand it when you do such completely stupid, lame, and ridiculous things! It makes me crazy!"), and act out her anger by slamming doors or banging her hand on the table to make a point. Scott, on the other hand, is usually very easygoing. It takes a lot to make him mad—but when he does get mad, watch out. He might express his anger in a calm, even a cold way, but he is very serious about his feelings, and it takes him a long, long time to get over whatever the fight was about. Julia kind of enjoys flying off the handle and then making up. To Scott, any kind of a fight is agonizing. Sometimes he feels like he'll do anything to keep Julia from yelling at him again—or to keep himself from getting mad at her. Julia doesn't understand what the big deal is—but she does hate Scott's cold words and long grudges. Sometimes she thinks she'd rather break up with him than go through another evening of his barely speaking to her.

Tina is one of those people who always says what she thinks. If she doesn't like you, she'll tell you, often with an insult or two thrown in. If she thinks you're doing something the wrong way, she'll say, "What an idiot! How can you be so stupid?" Tina is a very loyal friend, besides being funny, smart, and a lot of fun to be with, so she has lots of girlfriends and no shortage of guys wanting to go out with her. Her friends are used to her going on about how angry she is with this guy that dumped on her, or how mad she is at the new math teacher, or how frustrated she is with her parents. They're also used to her yelling at them or criticizing them. They know that if they object, she'll say, "I'm just telling you how I feel. What's the matter, don't you want me to be honest with you?" Sometimes, after Tina has had her say, she feels better—but her friends feel worse. Sometimes, Tina's insults provoke insults in return, and the friendship ends. Sometimes Tina *doesn't* feel better after she expresses her feelings—sometimes she feels even more angry, and nothing seems to help.

What do all these situations have in common? They all concern people dealing with *anger,* the emotion we feel when something seems wrong in our lives and we want to correct it. *Webster's New World Dictionary* defines anger as "a feeling of displeasure resulting from injury, mistreatment, opposition, etc., and usually showing itself in a desire to fight back at the supposed cause of this feeling."

How does anger come into the situations we've described? Theo's bad day is full of a range of anger-provoking situations—interactions that to Theo seem unfair (Why is his English grade being marked down so much for such a little thing? Why should *he* have to do laps? Why should his mother yell at *him?*) or hurtful (Why can't his girlfriend put him first, rather than preferring to spend time with her cousin?) or simply out of his control (Why should his boss have the power to ruin Theo's Saturday plans?). Theo is so angry about all of these incidents that he can't sleep—his anger is keeping him awake.

Mary Ellen, on the other hand, chooses not to get angry at situations that might make Theo mad. But despite her best intentions, she pays the price for not expressing—or possibly not even feeling—any anger. Since Mary Ellen can't use anger to help her set limits ("No, I don't want to stay home and baby-sit!" "Boy, I really hate it when you're late and you don't call!" "No, you can't change our plans at the last minute—I have feelings too, you know!"), her headaches may be the only language she can use to say "No," or "I don't like this," or "I want to come first this time."

Scott and Julia have very different styles of anger and very different ways of dealing with this emotion. As we saw, Julia is comfortable with expressing anger—but she does so in a way that makes Scott uncomfortable. Scott, on the other hand, gets angry in a way that Julia doesn't like or understand. He thinks she should have more self-control; she thinks he should stop holding grudges. She thinks anger is a passing storm; he thinks anger is the sign of a serious problem. Whether or not they are comfortable with their own ways of dealing with anger, they are certainly not happy about each other's anger styles.

Tina is angry a lot of the time, and when she's angry, she expresses her feelings. Sometimes this self-expression works for her; sometimes it doesn't. Unlike Mary Ellen, Tina knows how to set limits and say what she does and doesn't want. But some people would say that Tina's spurts of anger are like Mary Ellen's headaches—a way to control others and get her own way. People may do what Tina wants or agree with what she says just to avoid an argument, or, if they have disagreed, they may back down quickly when faced with her powerful anger. And, just as the headaches cause Mary Ellen a great deal of pain, Tina's way of expressing her anger may cause *her* pain. Sometimes the way Tina deals with her anger makes her feel worse, not better, especially if her expression of anger costs her a friendship or makes her own anger more intense.

Myths About Anger

In our society today, there are two major conflicting myths about anger. One holds that anger is a "bad" emotion to feel and to express. Scott and Mary Ellen may feel this way. They may think that people only get angry when they are selfish or out of control, that nice people don't get angry, and that certainly a good person should never get angry at family, friends, or other loved ones.

Another myth holds that anger is a "good" emotion to feel and to express. In fact, according to this myth, if you *don't* express your anger, you are being dishonest, and you may be hurting yourself, physically and emotionally—making yourself vulnerable to problems ranging from headaches, ulcers, and heart disease to anxiety, depression, and guilt.

In fact, neither myth is completely true. While anger is often uncomfortable—a sign that something is wrong in our lives, or at least, not as we would like it—it can also be an exhilarating and exciting emotion. Certainly, it is a *human* emotion, one that, wrong or right, is felt at some time by every human being alive.

On the other hand, it isn't true that the only—or even the best—way to deal with anger is to express one's angry feelings in every single instance. And even when it is helpful to express anger, there are a range of ways to do so, some of which may be disrespectful to others or may not be helpful to oneself, others of which may improve communication and closeness and bring relief. Therefore, it's important to learn how to *manage* one's anger—to be aware of one's feelings and to make constructive choices for interpreting and acting on them.

When You Bury Your Anger

People who believe that anger is a wrong, bad, or dangerous emotion may deal with their anger by burying it. That is, they simply refuse to recognize that they *are* angry. Think about the guy who raises his voice in an argument and then says, "I'm not angry, I'm just very interested in what we're talking about." He might be telling the truth—or he might be burying anger, refusing to recognize his true feelings.

Or take the girl who barely speaks to her date all evening. He says, "Are you mad about something?" and she answers, "No, I'm just thinking about a lot of things." She might really be preoccupied—or she might be angry, using her silence to punish her date, expecting him to figure out for himself what he's done wrong.

People bury anger in all sorts of ways. The person who is always late may be acting out of angry feelings. The person who is always having or causing accidents might be mad at himself/herself or at other people and acting it out instead of saying it directly. Forgetting about a date might be a way of expressing anger, as might developing a headache or getting into an unexplained "bad mood" while on a date. (We'll talk more about ways that buried anger comes out in Chapter 4.) People who bury their anger may not recognize their true feelings—but sooner or later, they find a way to act them out.

Of course, burying anger is not the same as consciously choosing not to express your feelings. You are not burying anger if you count to ten when a strict teacher scolds you or if you bite your tongue when your bossy Aunt Sarah asks you an annoying question. Counting to ten or biting your tongue shows that you are aware of your anger—you are simply choosing not to express it. This may be a wise or a foolish decision, made for good or bad reasons, but it is a different choice from burying anger. People who bury anger are feeling something without being consciously aware of it. Because they are feeling it, however, their feeling is coming out, one way or another.

What can be the result if you bury your anger? Here are some things we've thought of:

- bad feelings between friends and dates
- misunderstandings
- feeling depressed and hopeless
- headaches (sometimes migraines)
- stomachaches (sometimes ulcers or colitis)
- getting very angry at little things
- getting angry at someone who doesn't deserve it
- blowups—if the buried anger "explodes"
- making stupid mistakes
- reckless driving
- frequently being late
- feeling anxious or worried for no good reason
- feeling guilty
- feeling that you are a "bad person"

Can you think of other things that might happen when people bury their anger?

Of course, everything on this list can be caused by a whole lot of reasons. Buried anger may not be responsible—or it may share the responsibility with other events and emotions in a person's life. One of the tricky things about emotions is that people rarely feel them one at a time. Usually, they feel combinations of emotions—angry *and* scared, sad *and* worried, happy *and* nervous. Because of the myth that anger is a "bad" emotion, however, many people find it easier to recognize other feelings than to realize that they are (also) angry.

Sometimes burying anger can make a bad situation go on and on. When Theo's last girlfriend, Charisse, broke up with him, for example, it made him really mad. He told all his friends how angry he was about it, and when he ran into Charisse two weeks later, he told her, too. Then he felt like the relationship was over, and he could go on and find somebody else. But when Mike broke up with Mary Ellen, she felt sad for weeks and weeks. Of course, she really did feel sad, because she had cared about Mike a lot. But it was much easier for Mary Ellen to accept her sadness and say, "I miss Mike so much. I wish we were still together"—than for her to accept her anger and say, "I'm so mad at that stupid Mike! How dare he leave me? He's acting like a real jerk!" Because Mary Ellen was burying her anger in feelings of sadness and "missing" Mike, the feeling went on and on.

When You Express Your Anger

Some people have an easier time expressing their anger—but, as Tina and Julia both know, they may experience a number of different consequences when they do so. What can happen when you express your anger? Depending on *how* you express it, under what circumstances, and to whom, here are some things we've thought of:

- better understanding on both sides
- an improved or closer relationship
- relief

- discovering something new about yourself, your feelings, or your situation
- a feeling of power
- the anger goes away
- hurt feelings
- receiving anger in return
- receiving retaliation or revenge
- trouble in a relationship
- the end of a relationship
- guilt
- fear of what will happen
- fear on the part of the person who hears the anger
- the anger continues or even increases

Can you think of other positive or negative results of a person expressing anger?

Understanding Anger

Why is anger such a double-edged sword? Why does expressing anger sometimes lead to positive results and sometimes to negative ones? What's the difference between burying your anger and simply choosing not to express it—and how do you know whether not expressing it or expressing it is the right choice?

Of course, there are no simple answers to these questions. Different societies and cultures have different rules for anger. So do different families. Ultimately, every person must find his or her own way of handling anger, in himself/herself and in others. This book is designed to help you sort through your own feelings and make your own decisions about anger. It's also designed to help you learn to *manage* your anger—to make choices about when and how to express it in ways that will work best for you.

Anger is a human emotion—and human emotions are tricky. People often make mistakes in handling their emotions, whether they are feeling anger, love, fear, pride, or any other feeling. In our society, anger is a particularly troubling emotion because there are so many myths and rules about it—ideas that don't necessarily fit the reality of how human beings actually are. But with thought and practice, you can learn positive, satisfying ways to manage your anger. That way, when you choose not to express your anger, you'll feel happy with that decision. When you choose to express your anger, you'll do so in the way most likely to get you the best possible outcome. If you're troubled by feeling angry too often, too intensely, or too aggressively, you may find ways to defuse or work through your anger. And if you're troubled by feelings of buried anger, you may find ways to get in touch with your feelings, so that you can better decide how to deal with them.

The Uses of Anger

Let's start by looking at what psychologists and other experts know about anger. As we've already said, anger is a basic human emotion. Psychologists believe it's a very important emotion. Here are some of the things that anger helps us to do:

- recognize injustice
- fight injustice
- feel ambitious, determined to achieve a goal
- recognize a problem
- mobilize our resources against an enemy, a danger, or an obstacle
- set limits with other people, decide what they can and can't do to us or with us
- feel our separateness and our own individuality, allowing us to become more independent

Anger and Independence

Have you ever seen a two-year-old learning to say "no" for the first time? Mom or Dad says, "OK, Timmy, time to drink your milk now," and sweet little baby Timmy suddenly says, *"No! I Don't LIKE milk!"* Mom and Dad may be upset, but Timmy is thrilled and excited. He's just learned something new. Mom and Dad may want him to drink his milk, but he's not Mom! He's not Dad! He's himself—and *he* doesn't want to drink his milk. This may be the first time little Timmy realizes that he's his own person—someone who can say no, someone who can say what *he* wants and doesn't want.

Children get so excited at this marvelous discovery that exhausted parents (and older brothers and sisters) have a name for this age—"The Terrible Twos." That's because once a child has learned the fun of saying "No!" he or she may need to say it a *lot,* just because the discovery of being a separate person is such an exciting one. In fact, smart parents know that often, the best way to get a two-year-old to do something is to tell him or her *not* to do it. If Dad tells Timmy, "I don't think I want you to have any milk today," Timmy is just as likely to say, *"NO! Want* milk!" When children are first learning that they are separate people, that simple fact is almost more important to them than their actual feeling about the situation in question.

As children get older, they learn to express their anger and their separateness in different ways. Timmy may learn to say in a quiet, reasonable voice, "I don't feel like milk right now—I'd rather have juice, please." And, secure in the knowledge that he can ask for what he wants (even if he doesn't always get it), he may even be willing to take milk when Dad offers it to him. Now that he knows who he is, he doesn't have to say no just because Dad is saying yes.

This process of separation doesn't happen all at once, however. Learning how to know who you are and what you want is a long and complicated journey. Another big time of separation, independence, and becoming "your own person" takes place during the teenage years. That's part of the reason why teenagers often feel angry, especially with parents, teachers, and other adults. As teenagers struggle to figure out who *they* are and what *they* want, they may need to experiment with saying no to grown-ups, just to be sure they're finding their own answers rather than passively giving in to somebody else. Of course, this "no" doesn't have to be an angry "no"—some of the time, at least, it may be quiet and reasonable. But as young people are feeling their way, anger may help them feel the boundaries of their thoughts, feelings, and wants, *as opposed to* those of parents, teachers, and other adults.

Real maturity may come when you know yourself, period, not "as opposed to" anyone. But getting to that point takes time, and it seems to be part of the human condition that feeling anger is part of what propels us and keeps us on that journey.

Anger may serve another important function as teenagers grow up—it may help them leave home. Most young people feel *ambivalent*—two contradictory ways—about the idea of someday being on their own. They may feel excited at the thrilling prospect of becoming more independent, going off into the world to have their own adventures. But they may also feel sad at the prospect of leaving the people they love and scared about losing the security of being told what to do. Likewise, they may feel ready to make their own decisions—and also scared that they *might not* be ready to strike out on their own.

Some psychologists believe that anger may help teenagers deal with these contradictory feelings. After all, if you're mad at your parents—and at the other people in your house— you won't feel so sad about saying goodbye to them some- day. And if you're scared about being on your own (even if you're also excited about it), the anger may help distract you from your fears. You might be so busy being angry ("I'll show them! When I'm doing it *my* way, it will be great!") that you don't have time to feel scared or sad. That's another reason anger seems to be an integral part of the growing- up process—it helps give us the courage and determina- tion to "leave the nest," even if we also love the nest and the people in it.

Anger and Problem-Solving

Have you ever seen a tennis player have a tantrum in the middle of a big match? Have you ever wondered whether the player's anger improved or hurt his or her game? Jim E. Loehr, director of sports psychology at the Nick Bollettieri Tennis Academy, says that anger is often a useful tool for a star athlete—but tantrums are not.

Loehr has identified four main ways that athletes can respond to anger:

1. **Withdraw**—just pull back from the game and the competition. Clearly, this kind of response isn't helpful to anyone's game!

2. **Express the anger in negative ways**—have a tantrum, throw a racket, or blow up in some other way. It's true that this kind of anger may be a useful psychological weapon against another player, making the opponent nervous or uncomfortable. However, Loehr doesn't consider that good sportsmanship—and he doesn't think that having a tantrum helps a person's own game.

3. **Feel nervous**—a reaction that means that anger has broken the player's concentration. Now, instead of focusing on the game, the person is focusing on his or her feelings about the game, which have gone from anger to nervousness. Clearly, this reaction isn't helpful either.

4. **Have the "challenge response"**—decide to channel the anger back into the game, into a determination to play even better than before. Loehr says this *is* a helpful reaction, although, he says, it's something that many players have to *learn*. (Loehr's comments were quoted in an article by Roger Williams in a 1988 issue of *Psychology Today,* cited by Carol Tavris in *Anger: the Misunderstood Emotion.*)

The "challenge response" illustrates another important use of anger—in ambition, determination to reach a goal, and problem-solving. Anger is one of our body's ways to mobilize its resources. In fact, millions of years ago, it may have been nature's way of helping us to stay alive.

What happens to our bodies when we get angry? According to *Anger Kills* by Redford and Virginia Williams, and to *Anger: The Misunderstood Emotion*, by Carol Tavris, the biological reaction—commonly known as "fight or flight"—is actually a primitive response that humans developed in response to any danger. The chain of events involved in anger is very similar to that involved in fear, because both are responses to the perception that something is threatening us—something that we must either fight or run away from. Therefore, the body mobilizes to produce both fear and anger:

- The hypothalamus—a region deep inside the brain—is stimulated by angry thoughts. It in turn stimulates the nervous system to constrict the arteries carrying blood to the skin, kidneys, and intestines. If we were to get into a fight, or to be attacked by a wild animal, better not to have too much blood too close to the skin, because we might get wounded and bleed. And our body is directing blood away from kidneys and intestines, because digesting food is hardly our top priority right now!

- At the same time, the adrenal glands—located just above the kidneys—are sending *adrenaline* into our system, which causes the arteries that carry blood to our muscles to open up wide. If we really have to fight or flee, this makes sense—we need more strength in our muscles than anywhere else. At the same time, another chemical called *cortisol* is amplifying and prolonging adrenaline's effects on the heart and arteries—in other words, it's keeping our strength up for a prolonged response. That's nature's way of helping us mobilize our resources in case the fight takes a long time, or in case we have to run for miles to find safety.

- Meanwhile, responding to our adrenal glands, the hormones *epinephrine* and *norepinephrine* are also entering the bloodstream. These two hormones can be stimulated by any kind of *stress,* or demand, on our bodies: heat, cold, pain, bleeding, burns, and physical exercise. They also respond to drugs—caffeine (in coffee, tea, cola drinks), nicotine (in cigarettes), and alcohol—as well as to emotionally charged situations of all types: a person bumping into us on the sidewalk, a fight with a parent, a tryout or an audition, a big final exam. These hormones give us that tingle of excitement or energy that can go with any emotion—fear, anger, falling in love. They are part of the process that sets our hearts beating faster while cutting off blood to our intestines and digestive systems. That's why if you're very angry or nervous—or if you are madly in love—you probably won't feel like eating! (It's also why if you smoke cigarettes or drink too much coffee, you won't feel much like eating, either—nicotine and caffeine stimulate these hormones, which in turn depress the appetite.)

The interesting thing about epinephrine and norepinephrine is that a little of them goes a long way. An increased level of these hormones helps improve memory, concentration, and performance. But too much of them, and the balance starts to tip the other way: memory, concentration, and performance decline. That's why some people feel "psyched up" before taking a test or playing a big game, and they experience their excitement as helping them. Others, however, feel paralyzed by nervousness, and, as a result, they can't remember the simplest answer or make the easiest shot. Likewise, if you were only a little angry when your sister ruined your best sweater by putting it in the dryer, you might be able to remember every single word you said to her as you brilliantly told her off. But if, when your father yelled at you for yelling at her, you were furious at the unfairness of it all, you might not be able to remember a single thing he said—the hormones were interfering with your memory.

Here's another interesting thing about the experience of anger—and, indeed, of all human emotions: Some people enjoy the experience, and some people don't. Our bodies all come with the same basic equipment—muscles, blood, glands, hormones—but our minds have taught us to have different reactions to our bodies' experiences. Take two people getting ready for a big exam. Both have racing hearts, sweaty palms, and a tingling feeling in their stomachs. But one person experiences those feelings as fun and exciting—she feels psyched up, challenged, ready for anything. Another person experiences the same sensations as nauseating and depressing. He doesn't *like* feeling excited—he'd rather feel calm. Two similar sets of biological reactions—and two completely different mental and emotional experiences.

The picture gets even more complicated when we think of the different names the two people might give to their emotions. The first person might consider herself angry. "They think they've got me—but I've got them!" she might be saying to herself. "I'll show them—I'm going to get every single answer right!" The second person, on the other hand, might experience his bodily sensations as fear. "What if they ask me something I don't know?" he may be thinking. "What if I fail?" As you've probably noticed, some people are just more comfortable being angry. If they are scared, they may turn their fear into anger. Other people have the opposite reaction. Their own anger frightens them—and so often, their anger turns into fear. Often, the way we perceive ourselves, the world, and our emotions has a big effect on what emotion we feel—and how we feel about that feeling!

In giving us the set of biological reactions we've just discussed, nature has done its job. Clearly, we are equipped with many different emotions—including fear and anger— whose function is to help our bodies mobilize their resources to meet a wide variety of challenges. How we use those resources, however, is up to us.

In this context, it's interesting to look at people who have figured out how to make their anger work for them—how to use their anger to help them solve problems and accomplish tasks more energetically and efficiently. Carol Tavris, in her book *Anger: The Misunderstood Emotion,* quotes religious leader Martin Luther's description of how anger helped him to improve his performance: "When I am angry," Luther wrote, "I can write, pray, and preach well, for then my whole temperament is quickened, my understanding sharpened, and all mundane vexations and temptations gone." In other words, Luther experienced anger as sharpening his perceptions and focusing his concentration. Like the athletes who develop the "challenge response," Luther had developed ways of using his anger to help him focus on and solve the problems before him.

If you recognize these descriptions of anger as helpful and motivating, congratulations! You've probably already developed productive ways of managing—and perhaps even enjoying—your anger.

If, on the other hand, your anger feels more like an obstacle to you, don't worry. Jim Loehr has spent years teaching athletes how to use their anger productively. It's not something that everybody knows, or learns overnight—but it is something that everybody *can* learn. Like Jim Loehr's students, you can learn new ways of experiencing and responding to your anger, ways that will help you mobilize your resources and reach your chosen goals.

Anger and Injustice

One of the most common reasons that people give for being angry is the explanation "It just isn't fair!" or "It's just not right!" Sometimes the sense of unfairness is personal: "Mom said I could go to the party and now she's changed her mind. That's not right—she should keep her promises!" "All my other friends get to stay out till ten on school nights, but I have to be home at nine! It isn't fair!" Sometimes the sense of unfairness is more general, based on a perception that someone in authority is misusing his or her power, that a person or many people are being discriminated against, or that an innocent human being has been hurt for no reason.

If a person believes that he or she deserves bad treatment, he or she may react to such treatment in a number of ways—shame, sadness, self-blame, despair, resignation, even acceptance—but the person is unlikely to become angry. If, however, a person believes that the bad treatment is undeserved, that person is likely to become angry. The anger, in turn, can serve as a motivator to take action, to do something to end the bad treatment and right the wrong.

Think of the enormous courage that it takes to say, "Things shouldn't be this way. They should be different"—especially if everyone in your world seems to accept things the way they are. Anger can be a powerful ally, giving people the courage to speak up, to take action, even to risk their lives to work for what they believe is right.

Of course, anger doesn't lead to constructive action all by itself. An angry person may put energy into simply venting anger, rather than into coming up with ways to correct a problem. And of course, just because a person *feels* angry and ill-treated doesn't mean that he or she has actually been the victim of injustice. Mom may have had a good reason for changing her mind about the party or for enforcing an early curfew. Sometimes, too, even if a situation *is* unfair ("Why are her 'good reasons' more important than mine? *That's* unfair!"), it's not worth getting angry about. Still, in those situations where it's time to take a stand, anger can often help people see more clearly and act more bravely.

Misconceptions About Anger

Do any of these statements sound familiar to you?

- "I can't help it—I just blow up!"
- "I never know I'm angry until it's too late."
- "I always think of the right thing to say—afterward!"
- "I never get angry—it's not worth it."
- "Nice people don't get angry."

- "I got so mad I didn't know what I was doing."
- "He wasn't really mad—that was just the liquor talking."
- "She couldn't be angry at me—she loves me!"
- "If she knew I was angry, she couldn't take it."
- "How can I be angry at someone who does so many nice things for me?"
- "Look, I'm just being honest—so don't ask me to choose my words carefully!"
- "He didn't *mean* to hit me—but when he gets angry, he can't help himself."

In one way or another, all of these situations represent misconceptions—false ideas about anger. Now let's examine these misconceptions in more detail. According to various sources, including Gary Hankins and Carol Hankins's book *Prescription for Anger: Coping with Angry Feelings and Angry People,* and Harriet Goldhor Lerner's *The Dance of Anger*:

- **Anger isn't a mysterious force outside of a person's control.** We can't always control whether or not we *feel* anger. But we can certainly control how we *express* anger. People who explode in rage, who say hurtful things to others, or who use physical violence may want to blame the hurt they cause on their anger, as though their emotions have driven them to act in certain uncontrollable ways. But in fact, we always have choices about how we act, even if it doesn't always feel that way.
- **Being honest about anger doesn't necessarily mean saying whatever comes into your mind.** Feeling angry doesn't obligate you to tell another person about it. And being honest doesn't give someone the license to say insulting or abusive things. If a person's main intention is to hurt another, his or her goal is not to be "honest" but to attack.

  Of course, sometimes it *is* painful to hear about another person's true feelings—if the other person doesn't feel the way you wish. That's very different, however, from that person's speaking with the *intent* to hurt—and using "honesty" or "anger" as an excuse.

- **Drugs or liquor don't cause anger—although they may make a person feel freer about expressing anger.** In some cultures, people get angry when they're drunk or high. In other cultures, people get quiet, or cheerful, or fall quickly to sleep. What makes the difference? It seems that a society's beliefs about drugs and liquor have a lot to do with the way people act when they get drunk or high. In our society, alcohol and many drugs are associated with aggression—so people who wish to act aggressively may use these chemical substances to relax their inhibitions. The aggression they then express, however, is not the chemical's but their own.

- **If you know you're angry "after the fact," you can learn to be aware of the feeling at the time.** Often, people will realize "too late" that they're angry, or will think of a snappy comeback an hour or a day later. They may use this as evidence that they just "can't" express their anger about a situation while that situation is taking place. In reality, though, if a person is not aware of feeling anger until it seems too late to do anything about it, the delay is probably caused by the person's discomfort with the emotion. Not knowing about the anger until afterward may seem to guarantee that the person is "safe" from what he or she fears will happen if the anger is expressed. As a person becomes more comfortable with feeling anger (whether or not the anger is expressed), he or she often finds that it's easier to be aware of anger at the time, rather than afterward.

- **It's possible to be angry and to be a nice person— and it's possible to be angry *at* a nice person!** As we've said, anger is just a human emotion. Nice human beings feel it, along with pride, guilt, shame, envy, jealousy, fear, love, excitement, happiness, and all the other human emotions. And, chances are, the closer two people are, the more likely they are to feel angry with one another occasionally. We get angry about the things that matter to us—and so, the people who matter to us are likely to be involved in our anger as well.

Sometimes, when people are afraid of anger, they hope that being "nice" will protect them, both from their own angry feelings and from those of others. Unfortunately, though, people who are not aware of feeling angry are likely to express their anger in hurtful ways. Have you ever felt uncomfortable after what you thought was a compliment—and realized that the statement actually made you feel worse? ("Oh, you look so much better today than you usually do!") Has a "nice" relative ever given you a jacket two sizes too small—and then "nicely" suggested that you may need to lose weight? These are some of the ways that a "nice" person might express anger without even being aware of it. Certainly, it may be hard for others to realize that they've been the target of such a "nice" person!

Of course, a truly nice person works to be aware of his or her anger, so that it doesn't spill over accidentally into hurtful actions and remarks. Sometimes it's appropriate to express your anger openly; sometimes your anger may be better left unexpressed; but either way, even a nice person will benefit from being *aware* of his or her anger.

- **Feeling anger toward another person does not have the power to hurt or destroy that person.** The idea that our angry thoughts or feelings have the power to hurt someone is a very powerful myth that most people hold, often without even realizing it. That's because, when we're children, we really *don't* know the difference between thoughts and actions. A hungry baby cries—and a parent appears, offering food. On some level, the baby understands that she is small and weak and completely dependent on the parent. On another level, though, the baby learns to believe that somehow her hungry wishes "made" the parent appear. Then, when the baby or young child gets mad at the parent and wishes he would (temporarily) disappear, she may believe that her wishes actually have the power to make that happen. She may grow up with the secret feeling that her anger is really very powerful and can somehow hurt others.

Believing that our thoughts and wishes have an impact on the world around us is one way of feeling powerful and in control—especially in situations where we actually have very little power. This feeling may be reinforced by adults' feelings about anger. If the grownups surrounding a child are afraid of anger or get nervous around angry feelings, they may also be giving the message that just feeling angry can hurt someone else. They—and their child—may have trouble telling the difference between angry and hurtful *actions*—hitting, insulting someone, maintaining an angry silence—and angry *thoughts* or *feelings* ("It's not fair!" "I hate it when she does this!" "I don't *like* milk!").

In fact, as we've seen, everyone feels angry some of the time. And, some of the time, everyone wishes that bad things would happen to someone else, even to someone they love. Angry feelings by themselves can't hurt or destroy anyone. The only time angry feelings become a problem to others is when they're expressed in hurtful ways.

Thinking About Anger

Now that you've read the first chapter of this book, how do you feel? Excited? Interested? Relieved? Nervous? Upset? Angry? A combination of feelings?

Some people find it an enormous relief to find out more about anger, both in theory and as they experience it in their own lives. Other people find the entire topic upsetting, scary, or guilt-producing. Still others experience a range of emotions, feeling uncomfortable *and* interested, relieved *and* nervous, one after the other or all at once.

Anger can be a sign that something is wrong, a spur to solve a problem, a signal that we must take action, or a clue to discovering injustice. If you have strong feelings at any time while you're reading this book, you may be trying to tell yourself something, either about your own feelings or about something going on in your life. You may need to take some time out to think about what you've read, write in your journal, or talk about your feelings with a friend or a grown-up.

Most people in our society have trouble talking about, thinking about, and experiencing anger. If you come to terms with this powerful emotion, however, you'll be discovering a new and exciting source of energy in your life. Learning productive ways of thinking about and expressing anger can help you feel more peaceful and content with yourself while making your relationships with others closer and more satisfying. Best of all, you'll come to know yourself better, and to appreciate yourself as a fascinating human being capable of experiencing a wide range of emotions. This may not always make life easier—but it certainly makes life more interesting!

2

Angry Situations

There's a new baby in Theo's house. Sometimes everyone has fun playing with Keesha, but sometimes, Theo thinks, she just gets on everyone's nerves. Keesha has colic, which means that she cries more than most babies, and Theo is getting really tired of the sound of her crying. He notices how much more irritable he, his parents, and his little brother seem to be with each other, especially when Keesha's been crying for several minutes and no one can get her to stop. Plus, Theo's parents both work, and they can only afford a baby-sitter on certain days. That means that three days a week, Theo has to run home to baby-sit. None of Theo's friends have to baby-sit *their* brothers and sisters, and Theo thinks that his parents are being unfair to him. He feels bad about getting so mad at Keesha—after all, she's his sister, she's just a little baby, and he does love her—but sometimes he wishes she would just *stop crying*!

Mary Ellen is on her school's track team, which is on a strenuous practice schedule getting ready for a big meet. There's one girl on the team, Judith, whom Mary Ellen has never liked very much, but she always tries to be pleasant and cheerful with her anyway.

One day, after a long, difficult workout, Mary Ellen and Judith are coming into the locker room at the same time. Judith accidentally bumps into Mary Ellen and knocks her into a bench, giving Mary Ellen a big ugly bruise on her arm. "Can you *please* watch where you're going?" Mary Ellen says. "I'm getting really tired of having to keep out of your way all the time!"

"You're the one who's in the way," Judith snaps back. "You take up practically the whole aisle!"

"I'm not fat—you're the one who's fat!" Mary Ellen says— and then she's shocked at herself. She never says mean, insulting things—to anyone. What's going on?

Scott and Julia have just spent an hour alone together, kissing and making out. Now they're meeting another couple at a diner before going out to a movie. At the diner, Julia asks Scott if they can get two different sandwiches and share them both. Scott says, no, he doesn't like to eat off other people's plates and Julia should know that by now. Julia says to the other couple, "He's always like this—I don't know what he's afraid of. It's not like he hasn't already got all my germs." Scott finds himself feeling furious with Julia. He's so mad, he doesn't say another word to her the whole evening.

Tina's history class is a lot noisier than usual today—the classroom next door is being remodeled and the construction sounds are so loud that the teacher and students have to raise their voices. Mr. Rodriguez, Tina's teacher, is talking about the Great Depression. He tells the class that back then, there really *was* a shortage of jobs, unlike today, when people who can't find work are just lazy or poorly trained. Tina raises her hand, and when the teacher calls on her, she says, "I think that's so unfair. People today aren't lazy! They just can't find jobs!" Because of the noise next door, Tina has to raise her voice. The teacher also raises his voice, saying,

"You have no evidence for that opinion!" "Yes, I do!" Tina yells back. "Mr. Rodriguez, you are *always* down on poor people, and it just isn't fair!" Shouting loudly enough to be heard, she starts quoting unemployment statistics and other information, but the teacher interrupts her. "Young lady!" he yells. "This is *my* class, and you have no right to disrupt it! If you can't accept the information I'm offering, perhaps you'd like to visit the principal's office!" Tina is fuming. What right does he have to offer his information and not let her share hers? But she also wonders how they ended up getting into such a big fight so quickly—usually this teacher encourages students to offer their own opinions, especially if they can back them up with facts.

Sparks to Anger

What sets the sparks of anger flying? What kinds of situations can lead to angry feelings, angry words, or angry actions? Does it ever make sense to blame a person's anger on circumstances—a hot day, a broken soda machine, a long line, a careless driver? Can a crying baby provoke an otherwise calm person to rage?

Experts on anger tend to agree: There are no circumstances that *force* a person to get angry. What creates the anger is a combination of the circumstances and how a person views them. Certain physical and psychological circumstances—noise, a crying baby, frustration, interruptions—may make it easier for a person to get angry or may help intensify a slight feeling of annoyance into a full-blown loss of temper. But human beings are not just physical creatures. How they feel about a situation and what they think about it have a lot to do with whether they get angry about it.

Interestingly, this is not true of, say, laboratory rats. Various experiments with crowding rats into a too-small cage, subjecting them to loud music, or exposing them to prolonged heat will invariably produce "angry" reactions among these animals. If the unpleasant conditions continue long enough, the rats will begin to attack one another. Humans, however, will not *necessarily* respond this way, even though crowding, noise, unpleasant weather, or other uncomfortable conditions may increase the *likelihood* of anger. (These experiments with rats, and the differences between animal and human responses, are discussed by Carol Tavris in *Anger: The Misunderstood Emotion*. She was summarizing information she found in Robert A. Baron's *Human Aggression* and in an article by John Sabini published in *Violence,* edited by I. L. Kutash and others.)

In this chapter, we'll talk about some of the physical and psychological conditions that may contribute to anger. We'll explain what it is about those conditions that sparks or intensifies anger—and what perceptions and feelings a person must have about the conditions to turn a spark of irritation into a flame of rage. It's worth finding out about circumstances that contribute to anger because, as Tavris points out, when people understand *why* they're feeling aroused or provoked, they're a lot less likely to get angry. And if anger *is* the appropriate response, understanding the anger will help to manage it.

Physical Sparks to Anger

Baby Cries

Let's start with Theo's problem, a crying baby. Why does that sound so often provoke family anger?

Nature has equipped humans with a very important reaction to a baby's cry. When you hear that painful sound, your blood pressure automatically goes up. In addition, your skin becomes a more sensitive conductor of electrical impulses. These two sensations are physically uncomfortable—and they will continue until the baby's cries have stopped. Thus humans are biologically programmed to take care of crying infants, feeling uncomfortable while the cries continue and feeling relief when the cries finally end. This is nature's ingenious way of making sure that babies are taken care of. Males and females are similarly programmed, by the way, so that both sexes feel equal physical discomfort.

What we've just described is a basic physical reaction. But what relationship does that physical reaction have to anger? Well, if you know that whenever a baby cries, you can comfort her and stop her crying, you may feel discomfort, but little anger. If, on the other hand, you have a colicky baby or a child who is difficult to comfort, you may feel more frustrated. Will the frustration turn to anger? *That* depends on many more circumstances:

- Are you getting enough sleep? (Parents with new babies usually aren't!) Lack of sleep can lead to irrational thoughts and exaggerated feelings. A well-rested person might be able to reason. "Oh, well, we're in for ten more minutes of this and then she'll probably take her nap." A tired person may decide, "That's it! She's *never* going to stop crying! I'll never get any sleep, ever again!" Naturally, the prospect of a ten-minute annoyance will generate far less anger than the picture of eternal misery. The baby's cries may generate discomfort, but the anger comes from the listener's perceptions and thoughts about those cries.
- Do you have an accurate picture of how a baby operates? Some people have the mistaken idea that a baby's cries mean that the baby doesn't love her family, or that the baby is trying to punish someone. You can see how that view would contribute to feeling angry at this mean baby who is keeping everybody awake. But if it's possible to understand that the baby can't help crying, and that her cries are not meant as a criticism but only as an expression of her own discomfort, it's easier to feel sympathy rather than anger—even if you're also tired and frustrated.
- Are you feeling that the baby is getting too much attention or that you have an unfair amount of responsibility for taking care of her? If you perceive that the baby is part of

a situation that's unfair, you're more likely to feel angry at the unpleasant sensation caused by the baby's cries. But it's not the cries by themselves that are provoking your anger, it's the idea that you're the victim of injustice. In that case, you might rethink your situation. Theo, for example, might say to himself, "I guess Mom and Dad are doing the best they can. They really *can't* afford a baby-sitter. They're not being unfair—they really need me." Or you might take action to correct the problem. For instance, Theo might say, "Mom, I don't think it's fair that I have to come home and take care of Keesha three days a week. That's just too much for me when I also have to study." If you change your thinking and/or your situation, you're less likely to feel angry when you hear those piercing cries.

Of course, everybody feels angry at new babies some of the time. Even the most loving parents have moments of feeling frustrated, tired, victimized, and, yes, angry. Brothers and sisters also feel this way, even if they also love the baby. It's good to know, though, that it isn't the baby or her cries that are provoking the anger. Rather, it's our perceptions of the situation and our sense of whether or not we can do anything to improve it.

Exercise

What about Mary Ellen? What set off her unusual blast of temper? Would you be surprised to hear that *exercise* was partly responsible?

As we saw in Chapter 1, the hormones epinephrine and norepinephrine are released into the bloodstream whenever the body has to combat stress or solve a problem. Norepinephrine seems to be part of our cardiovascular response system, which helps regulate the body's reactions to doing hard, muscular work. Epinephrine seems to kick in when work "feels" hard or difficult—it's apparently more related to the emotional aspects of hard work than to mere physical exertion.

As we also saw, both hormones set the heart racing, close down the digestive system, and produce other physical reactions that help the body mobilize its resources to complete the task at hand. Since the "symptoms" of doing strenuous work are physically identical to many of the "symptoms" of anger, it's possible for the body to "feel" angry. That is, since our body's cues are telling us that we're angry, it's easy to interpret our physical sensation as anger. It's almost as though the body gets confused, as though it slips from one emotion into another, just because both emotions have similar physical symptoms.

Does working out *make* us angry, then? No—in fact, getting vigorous, aerobic exercise can help decrease a person's overall anger level. (For more about exercise and anger, see Chapter 4.) However, if an anger-provoking incident takes place *while* we're in a state of physical arousal, our emotional reactions may be more intense than they would be otherwise.

In other words, Mary Ellen wasn't feeling angry when she walked back to the locker room—but she may have been feeling slightly annoyed with Judith, whom she disliked. Then, when Judith shoved her, Mary Ellen didn't choose to focus on the fact that it really was an accident. She just got mad.

Mary Ellen's angry reaction—"Can you *please* watch where you're going?"—provoked an angry reaction from Judith, who responded with an insulting remark of her own—"You take up practically the whole aisle!" Now Mary Ellen has two things to be angry about—Judith's accidental shove and her deliberate insult. These provocations, combined with her physical state, help her to feel angrier and more worked up than she usually does.

Since Mary Ellen so rarely lets herself feel angry, she might also have been taking out on Judith some of her anger at other people. After all, she already didn't like Judith, so she might have felt safer getting mad at her, rather than letting herself be angry at Lissa or her boyfriend.

What if Mary Ellen had known about the anger-arousing effects of exercise? Suppose she had known that after a vigorous workout, she's more likely to feel her anger more intensely? Then, according to researcher Dolf Zillmann (who, with various colleagues, published studies on this topic in 1974, 1979, and 1984, cited by Carol Tavris), the effect of exercising loses its impact. Once you know that your heart is pounding and your blood is racing from exercise, not from anger, the confusion is over. Even truly annoying things—a shove, an insult—won't be as likely to set you off.

Sexual Excitement

Just as a vigorous workout can set your heart racing, so can spending time with a person you're attracted to. And, interestingly, your body may make the same confusing connection between that kind of excitement and anger. When Scott and Julia spent their warm and loving time together, they both felt excited—and that excitement gave an extra kick to the fight they had at dinner.

Of course, their sexual feelings didn't *cause* their anger. Julia was mad because Scott, in her opinion, was being a stick-in-the-mud by saying he didn't feel like sharing or trying something new. Scott was mad because Julia, in his opinion, was pushing him to do something he didn't feel comfortable with and because he felt she had embarrassed him in front of their friends. This fight was a lot like fights that they had had before, even when they hadn't just been romantic with each other. However, as with Mary Ellen, their physical state helped make the anger feel more intense, turning a routine quarrel into a bigger fight.

Frequently, of course, we have our most intense fights with the people we're closest to. Often we fight the hardest with boyfriends or girlfriends, for a whole range of reasons. We may feel most comfortable expressing our true feelings to someone we've been physically intimate with. We also may feel more vulnerable and uncertain with someone who knows us so well and could hurt us so deeply—and, if we're not comfortable feeling vulnerable, that might make us angry. If we came from homes where our parents fought a lot, being with a boyfriend or girlfriend might turn us into a mini-version of our mother or father, saying things we heard one parent say to another or expressing our anger the way we saw them express theirs when we were growing up. (For more about anger with people you date, see Chapter 3.) For these and other reasons, we're likely to have very intense feelings about the people we're dating—and anger in some form is sure to be one of those feelings. It's helpful to know, then, that strong sexual reactions can sometimes intensify our feelings of anger as well as our feelings of love.

Noise

When Tina raised her voice to disagree with her teacher, she may not have been feeling particularly angry. Just the fact of yelling, however—*sounding* angry—may have helped Tina actually *feel* angry. Likewise, Tina's teacher may not have started out being mad at his feisty student. But hearing Tina yell at him—even though he knew she was only trying to be heard over the construction noise—may have made him *feel* insulted and assaulted, since that's what yelling usually means.

As we've seen throughout this chapter, mimicking some of the signs of anger—in this case, raised voices—can actually help create the feeling of anger. Of course, if Tina had been passionately agreeing with her teacher ("That's such a great point! I have another example that proves exactly the same thing!"), probably neither one of them would have gotten angry no matter how loudly they were yelling. But once again, a minor disagreement becomes an intensely angry experience because of physical circumstances.

You may have noticed this yourself. Have you ever called out a question or request to someone in another room who couldn't hear you? The other person asks you to repeat yourself two or three times, and each time you use a louder voice. By the third repetition, you find yourself extremely annoyed, and you notice that the other person sounds annoyed, too. Even though you weren't angry—only trying to be heard—you feel as though you've been angrily yelling and the other person feels angrily yelled at. It's as though our bodies are giving our emotions confusing information, and our emotions are having trouble getting it all sorted out.

Being aware of this phenomenon is often enough to undercut its impact. Nevertheless, experts do recommend finding a quiet place for conversations that you know in advance may be difficult. If you have to raise your voice to be heard, it's easy to start feeling angry.

Of course, there was another element in Tina's story besides the noise. When Tina started feeling angry, she called her teacher "unfair," and she said that he "always" did the same annoying thing. No one likes to think that he or she is unfair, and it's upsetting to hear that we "always" do something. Tina's way of expressing her anger was almost guaranteed to evoke an equally angry reaction from her teacher. If Tina had said instead, "Mr. Rodriguez, I feel frustrated. I have a good point to make, and I'd really like the time to make it," she might have gotten a better reception, whatever the noise level. (For more on handling anger at school, see Chapter 3.)

Other Physical Sparks to Anger

What other physical circumstances can help spark anger? Psychologists and sociologists have pinpointed overcrowding, loud or annoying music, and hot, unpleasant weather as contributing to anger. Each of these conditions represents a stress on our bodies, and our bodies respond to these stresses in the way we've come to understand—by producing epinephrine. Higher levels of epinephrine seem to be associated with quicker and more intense reactions of anger.

Yet here, too, our interpretation of our situation is at least as important as the situation itself. If a crowd feels threatening, upsetting, or confining to us, it becomes a stress. A crowded subway or bus, for example, may represent a frustrating ride home from work or school, intensifying any anger we might be carrying with us at the end of the day. A crowded baseball stadium, on the other hand, might make us feel charged up and excited about all the support for our team. The subway car and the stadium might have exactly the same number of people per square foot—but one situation is unpleasant and the other is a thrill, because of the way we perceive them. In the case of the baseball stadium, the higher levels of epinephrine are experienced as adding to our sense of excitement and joy, not as contributing to our anger.

In the same way, in the case of loud music, one person's noise is another person's favorite group! You've probably noticed that, whereas you feel soothed coming home and blasting your favorite tape or CD in your room, the exact same noise drives your parents crazy. Likewise, if you were forced to listen to their music at a high volume, you might feel frustrated. Again, it's not the music itself that creates the anger—it's the feeling of not being in control of one's environment, and, perhaps the sense that it's unfair or wrong to have to put up with music you don't like. Feeling out of control or feeling victimized by unfairness can easily lead to feeling anger, with or without music. It may also be that, if a person is in a good mood, the music—however unpleasant—has no real effect, whereas if the person is angry or frustrated with something else, the music is an additional factor in intensifying anger.

Finally, hot weather has certainly been associated with short tempers. Police and government officials who fear riots or other urban violence get particularly nervous during long, hot summers. Once again, however, the heat is not creating the problem. It's only helping people to feel more intensely the anger they're already experiencing. That's why a minor incident that might be forgotten during the winter can set off a brushfire of anger during a heat wave.

Psychological Sparks to Anger

So far, we've been looking at physical conditions that foster or intensify anger—crying babies, loud noises, unpleasant music, heat, crowding, physical arousal, and sexual excitement. What about psychological situations—conditions that are frustrating, annoying, upsetting, or unpleasant? How many of the items on the following list would make *you* angry?

- a box of crackers so layered in plastic packaging that it takes ten minutes to get it open
- a soda machine that eats six of your quarters without giving you anything to drink
- a pay phone that doesn't work
- a long line at the store
- a driver who cuts in front of you
- a little brother or sister who runs into your room to ask you questions every five minutes

Now imagine your response to these situations in the following circumstances. Do you picture more, less, or an equal amount of anger?

- You've just come back from a long run, and you're *starving*. You go to get a couple of crackers to quiet your rumbling stomach—and it takes you ten whole minutes to get through all the packaging.
- It's a hot day, your car has broken down, and you've just walked a mile to the nearest service station. While you wait for the attendant to give you a ride back to your car, you try to buy a soda—and the machine eats all six of your quarters without giving you anything to drink.
- You've just finished gymnastics practice, and you're standing on the corner, outside the locked school, waiting for your Dad to come pick you up. He's about 15 minutes late, and you wonder what the problem is. Suddenly, it starts to rain, then to pour. You go to the pay phone to try to call him—and it doesn't work.

- You're giving your first big party this year, and you've gone to the store to get some last-minute things. Ahead of you is a long line—and the woman at the cash register has just asked the cashier to approve a check. It seems to be taking forever!
- You're driving near the city hospital—and suddenly, another driver cuts in front of you and turns into the emergency room drop-off area.
- You're trying to study for a big test tomorrow—and your little brother runs into your room with a different question every five minutes.
- You're trying to study for a big test tomorrow—and the phone keeps ringing every five minutes. First it's that new kid at school you've been wanting to date, then it's your best friend with an invitation to a party, then it's your boss to tell you that you can have the weekend off after all.

Anger and Frustration

How about it? Did your reactions to any of the situations change? Once again, it seems that getting angry is not a simple process of cause and effect. True, every single situation may still include *frustration*—trying to do something and not being completely or immediately successful. But, as you pictured the situations, some probably sparked more anger than before, and others less or none. Frustration doesn't necessarily have to turn into anger—again, it depends on how you perceive the situation.

You might be interested to know that each frustrating situation described above would probably start by setting off a similar biological reaction. Our adrenal hormones are responsive to stress, so whenever we run into a challenge or frustration—no matter how small—our body reacts. If, say, we have to open a plastic-wrapped package of crackers, and we have difficulty ripping the plastic, we experience a rise in adrenal hormones—our body's way of helping us to meet the challenge. When the problem is solved—the package is finally open—the hormones fall back down to a normal level. This rise and fall happens countless times each day, as automatic as a sneeze or a yawn. We only experience it as a problem when it's complicated by other reactions.

What turns frustration into anger? Well, in the case of trying to open the box of crackers, the combination of being hungry and being physically aroused from exercise might intensify the frustration of opening the difficult box. You might also feel more angry if you have the idea that you *deserve* those crackers—after all, you've been working out!—and that it's somehow unfair if you can't have them right away.

Likewise, the vending machine that won't give you a cold drink will feel more frustrating on a hot day, since your hormone levels are already up in response to the stress of the difficult weather. Add to that the challenge of coping with a broken-down car, and you may feel primed for anger. It may also feel easier to be angry at a relatively small problem—the loss of six quarters—than to face the fear, disappointment, and sadness about the huge repair bill that will probably come due for the car.

How angry you feel about the broken pay phone will also have a lot to do with other elements in the situation. If it were a beautiful day, and you were hanging out with a good friend, that same broken pay phone might be worth no more than a shrug and a suggestion to wait a little longer. If it's raining, and if you're already worried or mad about Dad being late, the pay phone starts to seem like an enemy—just one more obstacle between you and getting home. Again, your sense that you are being treated badly—by the phone, the rain, or perhaps by Dad himself—contributes to an angry reaction. Imagine how your feelings might change if the situation changed again—if, say, Dad drives up with your two best friends in the car and says, "Sorry I'm late, but I had to pick up your friends. I'm taking you all out for pizza!" Or suppose he shows up and says, "Your Mom had a minor accident. She's all right now, but we've been at the hospital." Either way, your anger at being left out in the rain would probably disappear or at least decrease, as you began to feel pleasure at the evening out or concern for your mother.

Now, suppose that while you're waiting, you *imagine* that the reason for the delay is that Dad is picking up your friends, or that he is taking your mother to the hospital. If these are your thoughts while you're waiting, would you be angry—at Dad, the rain, or the pay phone? Or would your thoughts lead you to have different feelings, pleasurable anticipation or anxious concern?

How frustrating you find the long line at the store again depends on the other feelings you might have about the situation. You probably imagined more frustration at the long line when you pictured having a deadline—needing to get home soon in order to get ready for the party. If, on the other hand, your boring Uncle Frank and horrible little Cousin Cedric were waiting for you at home, you might even welcome the long line!

Your frustration might also become anger if you believed that the woman writing a check and the cashier were somehow behaving badly. "How inconsiderate!" you might think. "How dare she write a check when there are all these people waiting! And that cashier doesn't even know her job—she's so slow!"

Of course, if you were feeling nervous about giving the party, you might also be more likely to get angry. Why? Well, you might feel more comfortable getting mad at two strangers in the store than worrying about whether all your friends will have a good time at your house tonight. Getting mad implies that you are in the right—*You* know how to behave in a checkout line! *You* know how that cashier's job should be done!—whereas worrying is connected to feeling that you might be inadequate—What if you don't know how to give a good party? What if no one likes you after it's over? It might be more comfortable to focus on your certainty that you know more than the woman and the cashier, rather than concentrating on your nervousness about knowing how to give a good party.

The example of the checkout line is interesting, because it also shows that sometimes we look for people to blame, people on whom we can focus our anger. If you're eager to get home because of your deadline and the line is moving slowly, you might want to find a problem—Why is the line moving slowly? Oh, it's that customer's fault! She shouldn't write the check now. And it's the cashier's fault! She should be able to do her work more quickly. Finding a problem suggests that there might be a solution. *If only* you could explain to the woman that she shouldn't write a check, *if only* you could encourage the cashier to go faster, then you could get home and have plenty of time to get ready for your party!

Of course, you probably won't talk to the woman or scold the cashier—probably, no matter how you feel, you'll wait quietly at the end of the line. But imagining that you *might* be able to solve the problem might make you feel that you have more control over the situation. Getting angry in this case is a way of imagining that you have more power than you actually do—the power to move the line. Accepting that there's nothing you can do—the line will move at its own pace—makes it less likely that you will feel angry.

Ironically, accepting this reality might even open the way to find other solutions that really might work. You could look around for another line. You could run to another store to make your purchases. You might even go to the head of the line and charm all the other customers into letting you go first. (Getting angry with the other customers probably won't be effective—but politely asking their help just might do the trick!) Accepting the reality of your situation might either defuse your anger or allow you to use it constructively. And if you decide there really is nothing you can do, you might find a way to make the time waiting in line pass more pleasantly—reading a magazine, chatting with another customer—rather than fretting and fuming and picturing the possible failure of your party.

The example of being cut off by a driver shows that our perceptions of other people's motives have a lot to do with whether we get angry or not. If you thought the driver who cut you off was just being rude, you might get mad. But if you believed he or she was taking someone to the emergency room at the hospital, you'd probably think, "Oh, that person has a good reason for behaving that way. They're not doing anything bad to me." You might still be frustrated that you were cut off in traffic, but you probably wouldn't get angry about it.

What about interruptions? Many people would agree that being interrupted is frustrating. But is it? And does that frustration necessarily lead to anger?

If you imagine studying for a test and being interrupted by your pesky little brother, you might feel frustrated. On the other hand, you might welcome the chance to avoid studying for a while longer—even fighting with your brother might be preferable to that. Or possibly your brother's questions are funny or interesting to you—or perhaps you even feel flattered that he looks up to *you* and wants to ask you about so many things. In any of those cases, the interruptions would be welcome, not frustrating.

If you imagine the interruptions as welcome news—the call from a potential dating partner, your best friend's invitation to a party, your boss's offer of a weekend off—they become even less frustrating. Now you're still being interrupted, but you're pleased with the content of each interruption. Your reaction is not anger but pleasure.

Anger, Fairness, and Self-Esteem

The point of discussing these various incidents is not to say that one reaction is right and another is wrong. Perhaps you didn't imagine feeling angry at any of the situations; perhaps you imagined feeling angry even when we suggested that you might feel another way. It's not helpful to say that anger is right or wrong in a particular situation—whatever you felt is true for you. What might be helpful, though, is to look at what elements in a situation set off your anger.

In all of the examples we've given, there are a few common threads:

- **People often feel angry when they think they've been treated unfairly.** If you think that the reckless driver who cut you off was just being careless, for example, you may see yourself as having been treated unfairly. If you think the driver had a legitimate reason for rushing—he or she was taking a patient to the emergency room—you may feel frustrated but you probably won't feel angry.
- **People often feel angry when they perceive that their sense of control has been undermined.** If you're in a hurry to get home to your party, and you're being held up by a long line at the supermarket, you're in a situation that you don't have control over. You might accept your lack of control, passing the time by reading a magazine or chatting with another customer. You might take action to regain control, switching lines or leaving the store. Or your lack of control might make you feel angry, perhaps at the cashier and the check-writing customer, perhaps at yourself ("I should have come here earlier!" "I should have gone to another store!").
- **People often feel angry when they perceive that their self-esteem has been attacked.** If you feel that a situation means something bad about you, you may respond with anger—at the situation ("How dare that stupid package of crackers make me feel clumsy and weak!"), at another person ("When Dad doesn't pick me up on time, it makes me feel like I don't count for anything!"), or at yourself ("If I was a better person, I'd have a better car that wouldn't break down, instead of this old heap of junk!").

Of course, different people have different ideas about fairness, control, and self-esteem. Some people don't expect life to be fair, and so they don't get angry when things don't go their way. Some people expect to be treated badly, and so unfair treatment doesn't necessarily make them angry (although it might make them feel despairing and depressed). Still other people recognize an unfair situation, feel angry about it for a few moments or a few hours, and then turn their anger into energy, taking action to correct the unfairness when they can, diverting their attention to other matters when they feel they can't do any more.

Likewise, some people are what we might call perfectionists. They expect themselves to do everything perfectly, and they may expect others to do everything perfectly, too. These people, as you might expect, become very easily frustrated when they run into obstacles, interruptions, and situations they can't control. Other people have lower expectations for themselves and others. These people are less likely to get angry when circumstances, people, or their own shortcomings get in their way.

We'll talk more about anger, personality, and expectations in Chapter 4. For now, let's remember that just knowing more about what might generate or intensify anger can automatically make many situations easier. If you know that exercising puts you in a state where you might lose your temper more easily, you're already far less likely to mind things that happen when you're in that state. If you're aware that one of the things that drives you crazy is waiting in long lines, you might make an extra effort to avoid those lines— and, if you do have to wait in line, you won't fly off the handle when a fellow customer makes a passing joke that wouldn't annoy you under any other circumstances.

Given the choice, most of us choose to blame other people for making us angry, rather than blaming circumstances, our own feelings, or our physical state. Tina, for example, was sure that her anger at Mr. Rodriguez was due to his insensitivity—and some of it probably was. But if she had known how much the construction noise was affecting her, she might have felt less angry—and she might have decided to take extra care choosing her words, knowing that both she and her teacher were being affected by a problem that neither one of them was causing.

If you find yourself getting angry, you might ask yourself, is it really the other person's behavior that's bothering me so much? Or is it just that I need to cool off, eat something, get away from this noise, or make arrangements for a quiet half-hour where nobody interrupts me? Just identifying what you're really feeling and what you really need can automatically make you feel more in control of your life. It can also make you feel better about yourself. It might even make your situation seem less unfair.

Perception and Reality

What should be clear by now is that anger is never the simple, inevitable outcome of any circumstance. Rather, how we perceive a situation, how we perceive ourselves, and what we expect out of life all have a great deal to do with whether we become angry about any given situation— as well as with how angry we become, how long our anger lasts, and how we choose to express our anger. We'll be talking more about perceptions and anger in Chapters 3 and 4. Meanwile, it's useful to remember that although we can't choose never to be angry, we have a great deal of choice about how, when, and how intensely we feel angry, as well as choices about how to *use* our anger to make our lives more pleasant.

3

Expressing Your Anger

A week has gone by and Theo is still fuming about his boss telling him at the last minute that he had to work last weekend. Theo felt angry about it at the time, but because he figured that he had to do whatever his boss wanted, he didn't say anything. That night, though, he kept thinking about it (along with all the other things that had happened that day), and he found himself getting madder and madder. Then he felt mad again when he set off to work on Saturday morning instead of going off for a drive to the lake. And when his friends came back from the lake and told him what a great time they had had, Theo felt angrier still.

Theo remembers reading somewhere that if you're angry, you should express your feelings. In fact, his mother once took an assertiveness-training course, and she told him that one of the things she learned was always to say something about your anger to the person who caused it. So Theo works up his courage, goes in to his boss's office, and says,

"Mr. Lundy, I don't think it was fair that you made me work last weekend."

"Well, Theo, I'm sorry you feel that way," says Mr. Lundy, "but I'm running a business here, and I have to do what I think best." Then he picks up the phone and starts making a phone call. Theo can't think of anything to do but leave. But now he feels angrier than ever. He's so angry, he would like to quit the job altogether, but he really needs the extra spending money. And it is a good job. Still, every time he thinks of Mr. Lundy just brushing him off, his blood boils.

Mary Ellen is feeling very uncomfortable around her friend Lissa these days. Three of the last four times they were supposed to get together, Lissa canceled, and the one time she did show up, she was over an hour late. She always has a good reason for canceling: One time, she didn't feel well; another time, her mother wanted to take her shopping, and she really needed some new clothes; the third time, she got a last-minute call from Greg, whom she's had a crush on for years, and Mary Ellen didn't want to be the one to get in her way. The time she was late, she had gone to church with her family, and then her father decided to take them all out for lunch afterward.

Mary Ellen knows that Lissa is a good friend. Last year, when Mary Ellen was going out on her first date, Lissa came over three hours early and helped her get ready. She brought all her own favorite sweaters and favorite jewelry with her, and she helped Mary Ellen put together just the right outfit. And when Mary Ellen spilled chili on Lissa's favorite sweater, Lissa didn't even get mad. She just said, "Oh, well, things happen—but did you have a good time?" Lissa is always doing nice things like that—but she is also always canceling dates and showing up late. Mary Ellen feels guilty even thinking negative thoughts about Lissa—and besides, Lissa couldn't help any of the times she canceled or was late. But Mary Ellen has noticed that she doesn't feel like calling Lissa up as often, and when they do talk, she doesn't always feel like telling her everything, the way she used to.

Scott and Julia seem to be having a lot of fights lately. Their fights usually follow the same pattern. For example, the night when Julia teased Scott about not sharing food and Scott got mad, he got very quiet and withdrawn. Julia kept asking him, "What's wrong? You're being so quiet! What's the matter?" Scott kept saying, "Nothing's wrong. I'm OK." Finally, at the end of the evening, when they were alone together, Julia said, "Are you mad at me?"

Scott said, "I'm not mad, I'm just disappointed."

"OK, why are you disappointed?" Julia asked.

"I think if you really cared about me, you would know what was bothering me," Scott said.

"Oh, that is so stupid!" Julia said. "This is just like you! You are *always* doing this, and I just can't stand it!"

"Fine, then we won't talk about it any more," Scott said.

"How can you do this to me!" Julia said. "You are so *impossible!*"

"Have it your way," Scott said. They go on like this for a long time. The madder Julia gets, the quieter Scott gets. By the end of the fight, Julia is so angry and frustrated, she's yelling at the top of her lungs, while Scott is barely saying anything.

Tina is feeling very low. She just found out that Marisol—whom she thought was a good friend of hers—is giving a party, and she, Tina, is not invited. When she finally asks Marisol about it, Marisol is uncomfortable, but she tells Tina the truth. "I still really like you," Marisol says. "But some of the other girls—well, they're kind of scared of you, Tina."

"Scared of me? Why?" says Tina.

"Because they know how mad you get, and what they say is that when Tina gets mad, watch out! I know you don't mean anything by it. But you know, they're more sensitive."

"What do you mean? I'm just being honest," says Tina.

"Well, you really yelled at Iris the other day," Marisol explains. "You told her that nobody but a stupid idiot would use hairspray in an aerosol can now that we know about the ozone layer. She wanted to argue back, but you just went on and on—she couldn't get a word in edgewise."

"I would have listened to her," Tina protests.

"Yeah, but you didn't give her a chance to say anything. And you were so sure you were right. And you probably were right. But it made her feel bad," Marisol says. "And when Madeleine wanted to go to that new Spielberg movie last weekend and you didn't want to, it turned into this great big fight. Madeleine's feelings were really hurt."

"I just said I didn't think anybody but two-year-olds would like that kind of movie."

"Well, Madeleine thought you were calling her stupid," Marisol says. "And she felt really bad about it for a whole week. *I* know you're just saying what you think. But they all think you always have to get your own way, and they don't like it."

Tina feels terrible. She had no idea people were reacting to her in this way. She doesn't want to stop being honest and expressing her strong feelings about things—but she doesn't want to hurt people's feelings and lose friends either. What should she do?

The Challenge of Expressing Your Anger

Theo, Mary Ellen, Scott and Julia, and Tina are all having problems expressing their anger. When Theo expresses his anger and doesn't get the response he wants, he finds it makes him angrier than ever. Mary Ellen feels that she shouldn't express her anger because it isn't justified and because she likes the person at whom she's angry. Scott and Julia each have very different styles of expressing their anger—so when they fight, each ends up making the other person even angrier! And Tina is finding out that her way of expressing her anger isn't working for her: It's hurting people whom she doesn't want to hurt, and it's driving people away from her.

Figuring out how, when, and whether to express anger often seems like an enormous challenge. As we've seen, people have a variety of mistaken ideas about their anger—ideas that often get in their way.

Theo, for example, seems to believe that *Once I express my anger, I'll get what I want.* It upsets him even more to find out that his boss seems to care so little about his feelings.

Mary Ellen, on the other hand, seems to believe that *Getting angry at someone is a punishment for that person, so I shouldn't do it if the person doesn't "deserve" it.* Because she likes Lissa so much and is grateful to her for many things, she feels guilty being dissatisfied with anything Lissa does. She may also hold the mistaken idea that *Getting angry means that someone has done something wrong.* Since she doesn't want to judge Lissa as "wrong," she feels unable to be angry with her. Mary Ellen also seems to be holding on to the myth that *If I don't say anything about my anger, it will just go away.* Sometimes, of course, that is true—but in this case, it isn't working.

Scott and Julia are each operating according to their own rules about anger, so naturally, they're finding it very difficult to communicate. Scott's rule seems to be *If I don't yell at you or say anything insulting, I'm not hurting you.* Of course, his silence is extremely painful—and maddening—to Julia. He also seems to believe the myth that *If you really care about me, you'll know what I want without my having to tell you.*

Julia, on the other hand, seems to think that *If I'm close to you, I'm allowed to say anything I want to you, including calling you stupid.* Notice that neither Scott nor Julia handles anger by talking about *their own* feelings. Rather, each finds ways to blame the other, accusing him or her of not being sensitive.

Tina has been operating under the mistaken assumption that *If you have a feeling, and you don't express it, you're being dishonest.* It's always good to express your feelings to *yourself.* If you're feeling angry, contemptuous, judgmental, or just not interested, it's helpful to know you have these feelings—that doesn't necessarily mean that you have to express them to other people.

Tina also seems to believe that *It doesn't matter **how** you express yourself, as long as you're honest.* If her purpose is simply to express herself, this may be true. If, however, her purpose is to communicate with others, then she may need to take more responsibility for how she chooses her words and how she makes room for others' feelings and opinions.

Making Choices About Expressing Your Anger

What are some more productive ways of thinking about anger and its expression? Here are some further thoughts about aspects of anger that many people often find troublesome.

"Justified" versus "Unjustified" Anger

Mary Ellen is like many other people: She worries that if she can't find a good reason for her anger, she doesn't have a right to her feelings. Often, people who are worried about justifying their anger feel very uncomfortable about anger, period. That's why they feel they need to justify or explain it: They believe they need an excuse for doing a "bad" thing—getting angry. If they can't find a reason or excuse that seems good enough, they try to reason themselves out of having the feeling. Or, if they are undeniably feeling angry, they try to find a reason for it that they feel comfortable with, rather than accepting that they may indeed feel angry for what sometimes seem like trivial, selfish, or otherwise unjustified reasons.

Instead of seeking to justify your anger, we believe that it's more productive to start by accepting it. After all, as we've said, anger is a human emotion. Everybody feels it sometimes, for all sorts of reasons. And, as we've also seen, anger has many productive uses in our lives. Our anger may be giving us a signal that something is wrong, alerting us to a problem or injustice, or helping us to become more independent and self-loving. If we can follow our anger to where it's leading us, we can learn a lot. If Mary Ellen, for example, can simply accept that she feels angry, she might open the door to all sorts of new discoveries about herself, her friend, and the friendship itself.

Suppose that Mary Ellen tried that approach. Suppose that her thoughts went something like this: "Hmmm, I've noticed that I don't feel like talking to Lissa as much as I used to. And I feel anxious and uncomfortable when she calls me, which never used to happen. What's going on? I wonder if I'm mad at her—is that what's making me not want to be with her? Yes, that sounds right. I'll bet I am mad at her. I wonder why."

Now Mary Ellen can start to figure out where her feelings are coming from. Notice that if she tried this approach, she wouldn't be seeking to justify herself, but rather to understand herself. Sorting out her judgments about her feelings and deciding what action she wants to take (tell Lissa? not tell Lissa? tell her what, exactly?) will come later. First, she just wants to experience her feelings and become aware of what thoughts are provoking them.

"So, I'm mad at Lissa," Mary Ellen might think. "I really like her—she's been so nice to me—but I *am* really mad at her. Why?

"Well, to tell the truth, I didn't really like it that she canceled our time together to go out with Greg. I *know* he's really important to her, but I should be important to her, too.

Am I just being selfish? Well, maybe so—I'll worry about that later. Right now, I'm feeling really mad at her, so I guess it's because she canceled our plans so she could see Greg."

Sometimes, just being aware of our anger in this way leads to the anger's disappearing. On the other hand, when we're not aware of what we're feeling and why, those buried feelings can take on a lot of power. If Mary Ellen buries her anger, she may end up feeling so uncomfortable around Lissa that the friendship suffers. But if Mary Ellen can allow herself to be aware of her anger without judging herself and to follow her thoughts through wherever they lead, she might find herself thinking something like this: "Oh, so *that's* why I'm mad at Lissa! Boy, it's good to figure that out. Well, now that I think of it, I'd rather have a friend that lets *me* cancel at the last minute if a guy calls—so I guess I'm not so mad at her canceling, either."

If identifying the feeling and the thoughts behind it *doesn't* dissolve the anger, Mary Ellen might need to explore her feelings and thoughts some more. "Wait a minute. It wasn't just canceling on me for Greg. She's canceled and been late a bunch of times—that time when her mother took her shopping, that time she didn't feel well, and that time when her family went out after church. That's a lot of times to change your plans! I guess this really does bother me."

At this point, Mary Ellen has figured out what she's mad about. She might go further and ask herself why—not in terms of justifying her feelings ("People *should* be on time— so I'm right to be mad when Lissa is late") but rather in terms of understanding them further: "Why does it bother me so much when she cancels plans? Well, I guess it makes me feel like I'm not very important. I start feeling like everybody else counts, and I'm just like this fly she can brush away. I don't like feeling small and unimportant. It hurts my feelings."

Now Mary Ellen understands exactly what she feels— angry, hurt, dismissed, vulnerable—and she understands what actions of Lissa triggered the feeling. *Now* she can decide what action she wants to take:

- She may want to share her feelings with Lissa, with the goal of getting Lissa to change her behavior. ("I feel really mad and hurt when you change our plans, so I'd really like you to try to keep an appointment once you've made it.")
- She may want to share her feelings with Lissa, period, without a specific agenda. ("I just wanted you to know I have a hard time when you cancel plans. I know you don't mean to hurt my feelings, but I end up feeling really hurt.")
- She may just decide to say "No" next time Lissa asks whether it's OK with her if they cancel their plans.
- She may decide that, after all, Lissa has the right to cancel plans, and she, Mary Ellen, would rather not share her feelings about that with Lissa right now.

Whether Mary Ellen decides to talk to Lissa or not, there's one thing she *won't* do, if she follows this approach. She won't tell herself that she's being silly, stupid, selfish, or bad for feeling angry with Lissa. Even if Mary Ellen does discover that something apparently small or silly is bothering her ("Lissa was only five minutes late, and I just felt so *furious!*"), she'll use it to find out more about what she's feeling and why, rather than to put herself down. For example, she might think, "Five minutes really *isn't* such a big deal. So what am I *really* mad about? I bet I was really mad about the last three times, when Lissa was much, much later, and it just hit me this time." Or she might think, "You know, I seem to be extra sensitive about being kept waiting. I don't really know why, yet, but maybe I should let Lissa know that I have a really strong reaction to that."

Punishing People with Your Silence

When Mary Ellen feels uncomfortable with her anger, she tries to act pleasant and natural—even though, as we've seen, she frequently doesn't succeed. Scott is another person who doesn't express his anger directly. However, Scott's anger comes through loud and clear—even though when Scott is angry, he never says a word.

To Julia and to others, Scott's silences are often more punishing than any insults or angry words might be. Of course, sometimes people get quiet because they just don't feeling like talking. People may be quiet because they're shy, preoccupied with other thoughts, worried about something, tired, or simply have nothing to say. But, as we've seen, Scott's silences follow a particular pattern. He gets quiet after Julia does something that he doesn't like.

When Scott stops talking, his silence is giving Julia a message. The problem is, since he's not saying anything, she has to do all the work in figuring out exactly what that message is. *Is* he really angry this time, or is he being quiet for some other reason? What is he angry about? When is he going to start speaking to her again? What could she do to make things better?

Thus, Scott expects Julia to do all the work of figuring out what's bothering him, rather than simply telling her. When he says, "I think if you really cared about me, you would know what was bothering me," he's actually punishing her by *not* talking to her.

By not telling Julia what's going on with him, Scott is also keeping all the control over when and how any problem will be resolved. If Julia doesn't know what's wrong, she can't express her own opinion about it—she can only beg Scott to tell her what the problem is.

People like Scott usually have many reasons for expressing their anger through silence. Some of their reasons may include wishing to punish or wanting to keep control. They may also be afraid that if they expressed their true feelings, their anger would be so powerful that the other person would be hurt or even destroyed. Their fear of anger may be part of why they shut down so quickly when another person gets angry.

Someone who gets quiet when he or she gets angry may also feel very vulnerable. Scott, for example, secretly believes that he will lose any argument that he participates in. Partly, he thinks that he just doesn't use words very well. Scott also feels vulnerable because being angry makes him feel guilty. His parents have told him that only bad people argue, so Scott feels guilty every time he argues with anyone. Still, like everyone else, he gets angry—so he tries to control himself by not speaking.

Julia's response to Scott's silences is a common one—she talks more. Then, instead of communicating about what either of them may be angry about, Scott and Julia become engaged in a power struggle. Can she win by getting him to talk? Or will he win by staying quiet? The more Julia talks, the more Scott feels frustrated, attacked, and guilty—partly because, in her efforts to get him to respond, she becomes more and more extreme in what she says. The more Scott stays quiet or squeezes out only a few words, the more frustrated and hurt Julia becomes.

How can they break this pattern? Of course, it's best if they both decide to communicate in a new way. But either one has the power to change the dynamic simply by changing the way he or she responds.

If Julia is feeling frustrated by Scott's silence, she might tell him how she feels, rather than attack what he's doing. Usually, Julia says something like "I can't stand it when you do this! Say something!" Instead, she might say, "It hurts me when you don't say anything. I feel punished and pushed away." Hearing Julia's *feelings,* rather than her demands for him to do something, might motivate Scott to respond.

If Scott continues to hold his silence, or to put Julia off with distancing comments ("I can't help how you feel"), Julia can inform Scott that she's not interested in having a discussion by herself. "When you're ready to talk, let me know," she might say. Rather than begging or nagging Scott to talk to her, she might simply stop talking to him. It might be easier for her to do this if she leaves physically, as well, after making it clear that she'll be happy to talk to Scott when he's ready to participate in the conversation.

Scott, on the other hand, might find new ways of protecting himself when he feels vulnerable and angry. If he could bring himself to say what's making him angry, he might be surprised at how much stronger he feels. For example, he might say, "Julia, I really felt embarrassed when you made that joke at the restaurant about sharing our germs. I think those things should be private." If Julia calls him "stupid" or tells him he's "impossible," he might say, "I stop hearing you when you call me names. Please find another way to tell me what's going on with you."

Scott might also find other ways to get the time and space he needs to deal with his own feelings. For example, if he really is uncomfortable about a topic and needs to think about it some more, he might say, "I'm not ready to talk about this right now. I'll talk about it with you soon, I promise." Perhaps saying that, and hearing Julia agree, would free him up to talk to her about other topics, so that he is no longer using silence to protect himself.

Or Scott might say, "Can we set a time limit? I could stand talking about this for just ten minutes—could we agree on that?" Then, when the ten minutes are up, he might say, "I really can't talk about this any more right now. If you still want to, we can talk about it again tomorrow."

Silence can be one of the most powerful messages a person can give. A warm silence can say, "I feel comfortable with you." A shy silence can say, "I don't know what to do next." Becoming aware of the messages within an angry silence can help both the message-giver and the message-receiver to find less punishing ways of expressing anger.

Situations You Can Change versus Those You Can't

Part of the reason Julia insists on expressing her feelings to Scott is because she believes that expressing her anger will get her what she wants. If she tells Scott about her anger, she expects him to care—and to express that caring by apologizing, taking back what he's said, fulfilling a request, or doing some other thing that he's been asked to do. Scott, however, may not want to do what Julia wants, no matter how angrily she expresses herself.

Theo also mistakenly thinks that his anger will ensure that other people do what he wants. When he finally told his boss about his anger at having to work that weekend, he expected his boss to care about his feelings and to respond by changing his scheduling practices.

In fact, there are some people who don't care whether we're angry or not, or who care far more about other concerns. Expressing our anger to those people won't necessarily affect their behavior, because our feelings, sad to say, simply aren't important to them.

There are other people who may care very much about our feelings—but who still won't do what we ask. Theo found that out when he tried telling his mother how angry he was about doing so much baby-sitting. "Mom," he said, "I don't think it's fair that I have to take care of Keesha so much. Can't we find another way? It really bugs me that I never get a free afternoon—I'm either at work, or I'm here with her!"

"Theo, I'm really sorry it's so tough for you, but right now, that's just the way things are," his Mom answered. "Believe it or not, I've tried to think of another way—but right now, we just can't afford to pay the sitter any more, and your father and I can't afford to work fewer hours either."

"We could afford it if you really wanted to!" Theo said. "What if I stop taking piano lessons? We could use the money from that."

"I don't think it's right for you to quit piano in the middle of the year," his mother said. "You said you wanted to study, and we've made a commitment to your teacher. You'll just have to accept that you have to baby-sit for a while. Maybe we'll be able to rearrange the schedule in three or four months."

"But I *really* don't want to keep baby-sitting," Theo said.

"I understand that, and I'm really sorry that I can't fix this," Theo's mother said. "But there just isn't any other solution."

Theo feels very angry and frustrated after his conversations with both his mother and his boss. Not only does he have the same problems he had before—obligations to work and to baby-sit—but now he feels disrespected and powerless, too. "Why doesn't anybody care about me?" he thinks. "Why doesn't it matter to *anybody* how I feel or what I want?"

Then Theo starts remembering the conversation with his mother again. He knows she cares about him. He remembers how sad she looked when she said there was nothing they could do right now. He *really* doesn't agree with her about the piano lessons—he doesn't think canceling them in the middle of the year is such a big deal, and he doesn't see why she isn't willing to do it. But he realizes that, even though she may be wrong, his mother does feel sad about the situation and sorry that she can't make things better for Theo.

When Theo remembers the conversation with his boss, on the other hand, he knows that his boss really isn't concerned about Theo's feelings. The most important thing to his boss is his business, and he's really not interested in how his employees feel about him.

Theo is faced with two frustrating situations: one in which a person doesn't care about Theo's feelings, and one in which a person may care but isn't going to do what Theo thinks is right. In situations like these, what should Theo do about his feelings of anger? It certainly doesn't seem to do him any good to express them!

Actually, if Theo gives up the idea that expressing his anger *must* lead to getting people to do what he wants, he may find that there are other benefits from telling people how he feels. And there may be other ways to use and express his anger—ways other than a direct statement of feeling—that will help him to get more of what he wants.

For example, if Theo can accept both that he is angry and that his boss doesn't really care about his feelings, he might still *use* his anger to help him think more clearly and to act more assertively. He can start by asking himself more about his feelings and his options. What does he really want—more time off or simply to be treated with more respect? How angry is he about what happened? Does he want to look for another job? Can he bargain more actively with his boss? What would happen if he said, "I can't work this weekend"—would he really lose his job? Would he be willing to take that risk?

After he's thought through the situation, Theo may decide that he's willing to risk his job if that's what it takes to be treated better. Or he may find that he's *not* willing to leave his job, so he may just have to accept that his boss is sometimes high-handed about scheduling. He may decide that even so, it makes *him* feel better to say, "I'm angry about this decision, but I'll go along with it."

A third option for Theo might be trying to bargain with his boss when scheduling conflicts come up: "I'm willing to work this weekend, but I won't be able to work next weekend." Or he might decide that he and his fellow employees should get together to push for another way of handling the scheduling.

Finally, Theo may discover that expressing his anger calmly and constructively leads his boss to think twice about changing the schedule. Expressing his anger to his boss may lead to Theo's being treated with more respect—even if his scheduling problem remains unchanged.

Of course, when all is said and done, Theo may decide that it's *not* worth expressing his anger to his boss. Even in that case, though, he's thought through his situation more clearly. And if he continues to feel angry, he can always try another option—looking for another job, or pushing—alone or with other employees—to change conditions at his present job.

Theo's choices about expressing his anger to his mother are a little bit different. That's because, even though she may not do what he wants, she cares about how he feels. Knowing more about Theo's feelings may help her to take his problem more seriously, to look more actively for other solutions in the future, or to look for other nice things she can do for Theo, even if she can't give him what he wants. Even if she's not inclined to change her behavior, Theo may feel better just hearing her say, "I wish I could fix it for you."

Sharing his feelings with his mother may also have helped Theo learn more about what her feelings are. Now that he knows more about how she feels and what's important to her, he may be able to look for other solutions that would work for both of them. Maybe he could arrange with a friend to share baby-sitting, so that the friend takes Keesha one day a week, and Theo takes his friend's little brother one day a week. Maybe he could agree to pay for some of the baby-sitting himself. Maybe he could find another student to take his slot with the piano teacher.

Even if expressing his anger doesn't lead to finding solutions, Theo may find that it helps him to feel closer to his mother. Being able to talk honestly about feelings brings people closer. Refusing to tell someone about your feelings is one way to make distance between you. If Theo and his mother can talk calmly and respectfully about his feelings— and hers—they may feel closer to each other, even if they finally can't agree.

Of course, Theo may decide that even if his mother does care for him, he feels better *not* telling her about his feelings. He may decide that he needs to feel more distant from her, that he doesn't feel like sharing his emotions with her. He may decide to wait until he feels less angry, or he may decide that this is one problem that he'll just keep to himself. Either way, it's important for Theo to know that there are other reasons to express his anger than simply to get another person to do what he wants. That way, he can choose the course of action that will feel best for him.

Accepting that there are some things in life that we can't change is one of the hardest lessons for human beings to learn. Feeling angry and not being able to take specific action about it is one of the most frustrating problems we face in this life. This dilemma is expressed in the following prayer, known as the "Serenity Prayer":

> Lord, grant me the courage to change the things I can,
> the serenity to accept the things I can't
> and the wisdom to know the difference.

How do we get the wisdom to know what we can change and what we can't? Knowing when we are feeling angry is often the first step. Expressing our anger—or choosing not to express it—is often the second step.

Ways to Express Your Anger

Once you've decided that you want to express your anger, how can you do so effectively? How can you, for example, avoid the trap that Scott and Julia fall into? These two people have such different anger styles that their expressions of anger frequently lead to misunderstandings. Or perhaps you're concerned about the kinds of difficulties that Tina has with expressing anger, when she finds that people are more hurt, upset, or intimidated by her expressions than she intended.

Here are some guidelines that may help you express your anger more effectively:

- **Be aware of the circumstances.** As we saw in Chapter 2, such factors as heat, exhaustion, hunger, crowding, noise, or having just exercised can make anger feel more intense. If you're experiencing these circumstances, you might take extra care in what you say and how you say it. In fact, you might consider postponing your expression of anger until you've cooled off, had something to eat, or otherwise improved your circumstances. You may not even be angry by then! And if you are, you'll be far better able to *choose* how you express yourself, rather than feeling driven by heat or tiredness.

- **Use "I-messages."** Rather than telling the other person what she or he is doing wrong, say how you feel. Instead of saying "You're driving me crazy!" try, "I feel so frustrated right now!" or "I'm so angry I feel like smashing something!" Instead of saying, "You're being really mean to me," try, "I'm feeling really hurt" or "When I hear those words, my blood boils." Telling the other person what he or she is doing wrong is almost guaranteed to evoke one of two responses: a defense ("I am not!" "It's not my fault!") or a counterattack ("Well, you're driving *me* even *more* crazy!"). Telling the other person how you feel gives him or her room to feel sorry, concerned, or sympathetic. A study by E. S. Kubany, D. C. Richard, G. B. Bauer, and M. Y. Muraoka, published in the fall 1992 edition of the journal *Adolescence*, found that "I-messages" got a better hearing than accusatory "you- statements," which tended to provoke and anger the people who heard them.
- **Be specific.** If something is bothering you, the more specifically you can say what it is, the easier it will be for the other person to hear—and the more likely your message will really get across. "I feel hurt that you're always late!" is harder to hear than "I feel hurt that you were late for our big date tonight." Avoid words like *always* and *never*—a person who hears those words just *has* to disagree, even if they're true!
- **Avoid insults.** It's no accident that words like *stupid, awful,* and *idiot* are known as "fighting words." When Tina uses these words in her expressions of anger, she may feel that they give her feelings extra power. Unfortunately, that extra power is just what her friends object to. Instead of hearing Tina's true feelings and opinions, they hear that she thinks they're stupid or that she's willing to

say anything to get her own way. They aren't listening to what she says—they're just feeling pushed around. Expressing her *own* thoughts and feelings rather than passing judgment on others would help make Tina's self-expression easier to hear.

Ground Rules for Fights

Dating partners or close friends may find themselves getting into fights quite often. These people may wish to establish some ground rules for their expressions of anger, to help make their discussions more productive. According to various sources, including Harriet Goldhor Lerner's *The Dance of Anger* and Gary Jackson Oliver's and H. Norman Wright's *When Anger Hits Home: Taking Care of Your Anger Without Taking It Out on Your Family,* useful ground rules include the following:

- **Agree on a time and place to talk about serious matters.** If you bring up something that's been bothering you on your way to an early movie, you'll both feel frustrated that you couldn't finish the discussion. If you choose a time when one of you is tired, or worried about something else, a discussion is likely to turn into a fight.
- **Make sure you're hearing each other correctly.** One useful practice is for each person to take a fixed amount of time to talk—say, five minutes. (Timing guarantees that one person won't dominate the entire discussion—or cop out by getting quiet and refusing to talk!) After the first person has spoken for five minutes, the second person must say back what the first person has said, in a version that the first person can agree with. For example, Scott might say to Mary Ellen, "I hear you saying that you're upset that I was so quiet all evening. You said that my being quiet made you feel hurt and left out. You said that I've pulled that kind of thing—been quiet all night—on several other dates, too, and that it's really hard for you." The second person doesn't have to *agree* to anything—

but he or she does need to listen and understand. After the first person agrees that he or she has indeed been heard, the second person gets a chance to talk, and to have his or her point of view repeated back by the first person.

- **Clarify your intentions.** Is your true intention to have your feelings be heard—or to change the other person's behavior? Are you more interested in working things out between the two of you—or in punishing the other person for the terrible thing he or she has done to you? Do you have a serious grievance, or are you just blowing off steam?

Most people have each of these intentions at some point in a relationship, and often, people have more than one intention at a time. If you can clarify what you really want, you can make better choices about how you express your anger. You might even share your intention with your partner—especially if you don't feel good about it. "I don't feel very proud of this, but I really feel like punishing you right now," Julia might say. "You've spent the whole night not talking to me, and I'm really hurt. I just want to get back at you by hurting you the way I feel you've hurt me." Telling Scott she wishes she could punish him is not the same as actually punishing him. In fact, if Julia puts this feeling into words, she probably *won't* be as likely to retaliate against Scott, and their discussion can actually bring them closer.

Connecting to her true intentions would also be a helpful practice for Tina. Before she launches into an outburst, she might ask herself what her real goal is. Does she want to score debating points, to change another person's mind, or just to make idle conversation? Is she more interested in picking a movie, hanging out with some friends, or expressing her thoughts and feelings about Steven Spielberg?

Asking herself what she really wants might help Tina choose words and a tone of voice that are more appropriate to the situation and that will be easier for her friends to deal with. And if Tina finds that she has surprisingly strong feelings for such a mild intention, she might ask herself what else is causing these feelings. Is she mad at these friends for some other reason? Is she feeling insecure? Is she mad at someone else and taking it out on her friends? (For more on understanding the sources of your anger, see Chapter 4.) Meanwhile, though, she can control her actual expressions of anger, so that she's not hurting people's feelings or bowling them over when she doesn't really want to.

Angry Situations

How do these suggestions for expressing anger work out in real life? Here are some pieces of conversation from a variety of angry situations, in which people try to apply these and other useful ideas to their own expressions of anger.

A word of caution: Nobody's perfect—especially when it comes to expressing anger! Sometimes we all say things we didn't mean to. And in the heat of the moment, we all might find ourselves yelling, "You stupid idiot—you're *always* screwing up!" Still, trying to express anger more constructively does pay off—so think about giving these techniques a try.

Anger with Parents

Marisol has changed her mind and invited Tina to the party after all. But now Tina's father has said she can't go. Tina is furious. She'd like to yell, "That's so unfair!" but she knows from experience that her father will just yell back, "I don't have to be fair! It's my house! Besides, life isn't fair!" So Tina tries another approach.

First, she takes a deep breath and counts to ten. She gives herself this time to focus on her feelings—she knows she's angry!—and on her intention—to get her father to change his decision. Tina says to herself, "I'd love to show Dad how wrong he is! But he'll never agree that he's wrong—he's so stubborn! What I really want is to get him to let me go to the party."

So Tina tries to find out more about her father's position. First she lets him know she's heard him. "OK, Dad, I understand that you don't want me to go to the party."

"You're darn right I don't."

"But why don't you want me to go?" Tina asks.

"You know why! I don't have to explain myself to you!" her father says.

"I understand that you don't want me to go," Tina repeats. "But I'd really appreciate it if you'd tell me why."

"I don't know who those people are," Tina's father explains. "But I know they live in a bad neighborhood. And I know you, Tina. You're always staying out late. I don't trust you. You would tell me you'd be home on time, and then you'd be out till all hours."

Tina is really tempted to lose her temper and start yelling. How can her father say those unfair things about her? She's not *always* late! And how dare he not trust her friends, just because he doesn't like where they live? But Tina really wants to go to the party, so she reminds herself again that it doesn't matter who is right or wrong. What matters is getting her dad's permission. Once again, she focuses her anger on achieving her intention.

She decides that, rather than argue with her father, she'll try to put them both on the same side. She'll present the situation as a problem and ask her father if they can solve it together. "I know you're concerned about my being safe," she says. "What would it take to make you feel OK about that?"

"I already told you—don't go to the party!" her father says.

"I know you don't want me to go," Tina says. "But is there anything I could do that would make you not feel worried? Would it help if I *promised* to be back on time? Would it help if I put it in writing? I'd really like to go to that party—can't you help me figure out a way where I could go and you wouldn't be worried?"

"I don't know," says Tina's father. "I still don't know anything about these people."

Tina *really* doesn't want to make this next suggestion—but she decides that if she gets to go to the party, it's worth it. So she says, "Would it make you feel better if I had Marisol's mother call you up? She's really nice—you'd like her—would that help?"

"I don't know," Tina's father says again. Tina can tell he's wavering. Part of her wants to yell, "I shouldn't have to go through all this just to go to a party!" But again, she uses her anger to focus on what she really wants. She tries to show her father that she hears his concerns and is responding to them.

"So if I have Marisol's mom call you up, and if I *promise* to be back by ten, and if I put that promise in writing—would that make you feel better?"

"Maybe it would. I'll think about it," Tina's father says. Tina realizes that right now, she should back off. Otherwise, her father might feel that proving he's in charge is more important than anything else. She'll let him think this over, and maybe he'll say yes the next time she brings it up. Because Tina kept her temper, she has given her father a chance to move away from his anger, too.

Here are some other ways of expressing anger to parents. What kind of responses do you think these approaches might get:

- "I know you need my help around the house, and I'm willing to help. But I feel so frustrated—I don't have enough time to see my friends!"
- "I hate being teased!"
- "What you just said really hurt my feelings."
- "Right now, I'm feeling like nobody is listening to me or taking me very seriously. It's kind of a lonely feeling."
- "When you interrupt me, I forget what I wanted to say. If I promise not to interrupt you, would you promise not to interrupt me?"

- "I get that you're upset with me right now—and I'm upset, too! What would make you feel better?"

(For more on anger with parents, see Chapter 4.)

Anger with Brothers and Sisters

The relationship with a brother or a sister can be difficult even if you are also close. In fact, sometimes it seems that the relationship is difficult *because* it is so close. Anger can emerge in these relationships for many reasons:

- to try to make some distance inside such a close relationship
- as a way of testing power
- out of competition for parents' attention or resources
- as part of the inevitable stresses and strains of living together

Frequently, fights between brothers and sisters turn into fierce power struggles, where *what* is being fought over becomes far less important than *who* wins the fight. The problem with this type of argument, though, is that no one ever really wins. The "loser" is usually so angry and hurt about being kept out of power that he or she often vows to *retaliate,* to get revenge at the next possible opportunity.

Is it possible to express anger with a brother or sister while avoiding that type of power struggle? Yes, if you keep these two points in mind:

- You have a right to set limits.
- You'll be more effective if you express your own feelings, rather than focusing on what the other person has done wrong.

Knowing that you have a right to set limits means that sometimes you can walk away from a fight. As Tina learned when fighting with her father, sometimes it's more important to get what you want than to prove that you're right. If you feel entitled to be treated well, if you take your right to good treatment for granted and don't have to *defend* it, you may sometimes choose to walk away from a brother or sister who seems to be treating you badly. Or you might be willing to offer a compromise (even if you wish you didn't have to!), or to ask the brother or sister to work with you to find a solution.

Here are some ways of expressing anger to brothers and sisters. What kind of response might they evoke?

- "You know, that kind of teasing just makes me feel lousy."
- "I see that you've spilled grape juice all over my sweater that you borrowed, and I'm just boiling! That's my favorite sweater! I'm really going to miss it! I feel terrible!"
- "I know you like playing that music, but I really don't like it. The room belongs to both of us. What do you think we should do?"
- "I don't talk to people who talk to me that way. When you're ready to be polite, then we'll talk."

Anger with Friends

It's often hard to express anger to our friends. Sometimes we feel even closer to them than to our families, and so we may feel that we need them too much to risk expressing anger. Yet friends who are important to us will almost certainly also be the targets of our anger, precisely because they *are* important to us, and so what they do matters.

When expressing anger to a friend, it might be useful to keep the following points in mind:

You may need to express your anger even if you believe it is unjustified. If your anger with a friend is getting in the way of a friendship, talking about it might help bring you closer, even if the situation doesn't change:

- "I know it's a little thing, but it really bothers me when you tease me about the people I have crushes on."
- "I feel bad about this, but when you go off with Marisol, I get mad that you're leaving me out. I don't think you're doing anything wrong—but I feel angry anyway."
- "For some reason, I've been really annoyed with you lately. You're a good friend, and I don't like feeling that way."

If you possibly can, try to separate how you're feeling from what you want your friend to do. Just expressing your feelings with no demands attached gives your friend a chance to focus on the situation, with no chance to say no to your request. Perhaps your friend will offer his or her own solution to the problem. Perhaps your friend will ask you what you'd like him or her to do. Or perhaps you can bring up your request later in the conversation:

- "It makes me feel impatient and nervous when you're late, and then I get angry." (Later, you might say: "Would you be willing to make an extra effort to be on time? Or would you at least call if you're going to be late?")
- "When you say you'll call and you don't, it really bugs me." (Later, you might say: "I'd really appreciate your being careful about what you say you're going to do.")
- "I heard that you told Terry that I talk too much, and I'm really ticked off! I *hate* being talked about behind my back!" (Later, you might say: "I need to know you're a loyal friend.")

Remember that your friend is on *your* side—he or she is not an enemy! You can expect a friend to care about your feelings, and you can ask him or her to help you find solutions that will work for both of you. (If your friend seems not to care about your feelings, you might decide to reevaluate the friendship.) Here are some possible ways of asking for help:

- "I'm really upset about this—what do you think we could do?"
- "I don't like feeling angry with you all the time. How can we make this work better?"
- "How can we fix this?"

Anger with Dating Partners

As we've seen, dating relationships often spark a lot of anger. That's because they're likely to make us feel vulnerable—a feeling that many people find uncomfortable. We also tend to care a great deal about how the people we date behave, and that caring can lead to anger when they disappoint us or don't do what we'd like.

The suggestions for handling anger with friends work for anger with dating partners as well. In addition, if you've been going out for a while, you and the person you're dating might want to agree on ground rules for talking about the things that bother you. (See the previous section.)

Here are a few other suggestions for bringing up anger with dating partners:

Talking about your own feelings, rather than saying what the other person has done wrong.

- Instead of "You're so selfish!" try saying, "I'm feeling really left out" or "I'm feeling short-changed."
- Instead of "Why are you being mean to me?" try saying, "My feelings are really hurt" or "I'm feeling really insulted—and it's ticking me off!"
- Instead of "Stop nagging!" try saying "I'm feeling like I can't do anything right," or "It's so frustrating—as soon as I've done one thing, I feel like I'm supposed to start on the next!"

If you do talk about the other person, describe his or her *behavior*, not *character*.

- Instead of "You're so inconsiderate," try, "You were late today, and that drives me crazy!"
- Instead of "You're so selfish," try, "I feel so left out—we were out together for a whole evening and you only spoke to me a couple of times."
- Instead of "You're so unreasonable," try, "I just finished taking you out to a movie, and you're already asking me when we can see each other again. I feel like however much I do, it's not enough."

If you talk about the other person's behavior, be *specific*, not *general*. Avoid words like "never" and "always."

- Instead of "You're always late," try, "You were late for our date today, and you've been late two or three times more this past month."
- Instead of "You never talk to me," try, "We were out for a whole evening, and the only time I remember your asking me a question was when the waitress came to take our order and you asked me what I wanted."

When possible, say what you *do* want instead of what you *don't* want. But say it specifically. Telling someone you want him or her to be "better" will only make them nervous that they can't measure up—and their nervousness may make them angry.

- Instead of "You never talk to me," try, "There are all these things I want to share with you—when can I do that?" or "I don't even know what's going on with you at school, or with your family, or with your friends—I'd like to hear more about your life."
- Instead of "You're so inconsiderate," try, "It would make me feel great if you could call me when something big is going on for me, just to find out how I am. Is that something you could do?"

Anger at School or at Work

Most people have the most difficulty expressing anger to people who are in positions of authority—people like employers, teachers, and principals. People's difficulties tend to come out in one of two ways: either they swallow their anger completely, believing in advance that they can't win anyway or that they're in danger of punishment; or their sense of being "on the bottom" pushes them to express their anger in even more extreme ways than they would with someone "on their own level."

Ironically, these very different ways of expressing anger might both be coming from the same feeling. In both cases, people might start out feeling that "They're so powerful—it makes me feel small and helpless." A more cautious person might decide, "They're so powerful—I guess I really *am* small and helpless—nothing I do will make any difference." A more insistent person might decide, "They're so powerful—I *hate* feeling small and helpless—how dare they make me feel this way?—I'd better speak in a very loud voice so I'll be heard." Both types of people, though, may be forgetting about their own power and their own ability to decide for themselves what they want to do.

If something at school or at work is making you angry, you may *not* be able to change it—and you may need to accept that, sooner or later. Perhaps, though, you *will* be able to change it, or to change part of it, or to change your relationship to it. If you really believe Ms. Myers is a terrible teacher, you might not be able to improve *her*—but maybe you can get transferred into another class. If Mr. Rodriguez has a habit of baiting or insulting students, and then punishing them for talking back, you may have to learn a way not to rise to the bait while still keeping your dignity. If your boss has a habit of making you wait a few extra days for your paycheck, you may or may not be able to change his behavior—but it might make you feel better to express your anger and your sense that he's acting unfairly.

The key in all these cases is in *using* your anger, rather than letting your anger use you. Stay focused on what you want, and keep your judgment sharp about what is actually going on. Here are some other suggestions:

- Say what the problem is, calmly and clearly. Be specific. "The other day in class, I had a point to make, but you wouldn't let me talk."
- Acknowledge the other person's position. "I know you have to keep the class moving, and that you want us to hear what you have to say."
- Say what you want. "But I'd really like it if somehow I could say what I think, too."
- Ask for the other person's help in solving the problem. "Is there any way I could do that that would work for you?"

Here's how Theo used that technique to talk to his boss:

- **He said what the problem was:** "Last week, you had given me the schedule, and I made my plans based on it. Then, at the last minute, you changed the schedule."
- **He acknowledged the other person's position:** "I know you have to make sure there are people here all the time."
- **He said what he wanted:** "But I really need to know when I'm working and when I'm not, so I can make other plans."
- **He asked for his boss's help in solving the problem:** "Is there any way you can make sure people are here— and still give me more notice?"

Anger with Strangers

Handling anger with strangers is somewhat different from other situations, because you don't usually have an ongoing relationship with strangers. As a result, people often handle their anger in a different way with strangers than with those they know. They may feel unusually timid about standing up for themselves ("I can get angry with Alison because I know her, but how can I get angry with this waitress who keeps ignoring me?") or they may feel exceptionally free to vent their anger ("I'll never see that clerk again—why shouldn't I tell him what I think of him?"). Neither reaction is likely to be particularly helpful.

What things *are* important to keep in mind when feeling angry with strangers? We suggest the following:

- **Make sure you take care of yourself.** As we've seen, anger can be a powerful ally in helping you to set limits, correct an injustice, and get what you want. If a stranger does something to make you angry, your feelings may inspire you to stand up for yourself and make sure you've been treated appropriately.
- **Live up to your own standards.** How do you think people *should* be treated? Do you believe that it's important to treat others with courtesy and respect? If so, you can make sure that you treat strangers properly, even if you're angry with them, or angry about some problem that you need them to solve. As we've seen, getting angry doesn't have to mean losing your temper or venting your harshest feelings. You only need to be aware of your feelings. However you choose to handle your anger with a stranger, you can always act as though both you and the other person have a right to dignity.

Choose the most effective way to express your feelings and your wishes:

- As with friends, parents, and others whom you know, "I-messages" are likely to be heard and responded to better than accusatory statements: "I'm feeling very frustrated here," rather than, "You're really screwing this up."
- It's helpful to be specific and to avoid exaggeration: "I've been waiting for my sandwich for half an hour," rather than, "I've been sitting here all morning!"

- Telling someone exactly what you want, in a straightforward and non-accusatory way, is often effective as well: "I'd like my cola right now, and my sandwich as soon as possible, please," or "Could you please find out how much longer my food will be?" rather than, "How long do I have to wait, already?"
- In the same vein, it's sometimes helpful to explain *why* you're so insistent: "I've got to be at a doctor's appointment in fifteen minutes, so I need to know whether I should wait for my order or leave now," rather than, "I haven't got all day, you know!"
- Whenever possible, acknowledge the other person's point of view, particularly if they are not responsible for the situation that's making you angry: "I realize you've checked with the cook three times already," or "I can see how busy you are," rather than, "God, the service in this restaurant is terrible!"
- Use humor or exaggeration to help get the other person on your side: "You know, there must be 20 customers in here, and I bet every one of them has to be somewhere 5 minutes ago! Maybe they expect you to serve them at the speed of light!"

People who feel frustrated in angry situations involving strangers usually make one of two mistakes. Either they decide that they and their own feelings are not important and simply suppress their own needs or they get sucked into wanting to *win* above all else.

People who suppress their own needs may feel pushed around by strangers. It may be hard for them to tell a waiter that he has brought them the wrong order, to return a defective product to a store, or to face a rude or preoccupied clerk.

People who need to *win* may also feel pushed around—but they're determined to push back! They may find that the venting of their anger doesn't actually improve the way strangers treat them. Nor, perhaps, do they feel any better when their venting is over: They aren't being treated with any more respect, and expressing their anger hasn't really changed their situation. In fact, it may even make things worse by provoking the annoying stranger to act even more rudely than before, just to prove that he or she also refuses to be pushed around.

Take the example of a person who has gone to City Hall to correct an error on a driver's license. Which of these three approaches do you think is likely to get the best response? Which would *you* be most likely to use? Would that approach work for you?

- "Hey, somebody really screwed up here! You've got my birthday all wrong—it looks like I'm only eleven. You'd better fix it soon!"
- Could you take a look at this please? I think someone made a mistake."
- "I'm so frustrated! I know you're not the one who made the mistake, but can you help me fix this? Someone put the wrong date on my driver's license, and I can't drive until it's changed. (laughing) I *know* I look older than eleven!"

In our opinion, a response like the last one is probably going to be the most effective. Notice how it leaves plenty of room for the other person. It doesn't seek to place blame, to put the other person in the wrong, or to criticize. Rather, it acknowledges the other person's point of view, says clearly what is needed to correct the situation, and leaves room for both people to be right.

Sometimes, once you realize you're angry, you can then move on to defuse your anger—making a joke to yourself, renewing your faith in the other person's good will, bringing a note of warmth or human connection into an otherwise angry, impersonal, or alienating situation. At the same time, the initial realization of your anger can move you to act on your own behalf. Try smiling or joking with the hassled waitress—while asking her to check on your order; or try acknowledging that the broken air-conditioning in the driver's license office is probably bothering the clerk more than it's bothering you—while still pressing the clerk to correct your license. You may find that the waitress perks up and gives you royal treatment, or that the clerk, however charming you are, treats you like an exasperating nuisance. Being in touch with your anger—and being willing to let go of it—can help you allocate your time, energy, and charm in ways that make *your* day go better, at least—no matter how other people choose to respond to you.

As we've seen, anger is a volatile and powerful emotion. Using your own anger to help you get more of what you want from strangers—whether what you want is a specific service or simply more respect—can be a positive and empowering experience.

Accepting Your Feelings

As we've said before, people have a wide range of feelings about their emotions. Some people enjoy being angry; others feel guilty, ashamed, out of control, or depressed by their own anger. However, you feel about your anger, though, you can learn to express it in productive and effective ways—it just takes practice? And you may also find that the more comfortable you become expressing your anger productively, the better able you are to accept your anger along with all the rest of your feelings.

4

Coping with Your Anger

Theo has been feeling really frustrated lately. He seems to be angry at a lot of people a lot of the time. Everyone seems to be getting on his nerves—his little brother, his baby sister Keesha, his mother, his boss, his girlfriend. When he thinks about it, Theo has the feeling that some of his anger is justified, and some of it isn't. Knowing that doesn't seem to matter, however—he's still angry and dissatisfied a lot of the time. Sometimes his anger comes out in angry words, or in yelling, or in his stalking away to his room and slamming the door. Sometimes Theo sits on his anger, biting his tongue and not saying anything. When he vents his anger, he feels frustrated and, sometimes, guilty and ashamed. When he swallows his anger, he also feels frustrated, and, usually, helpless and depressed. Theo feels that his anger is like a tangled net that restricts him and pulls at him every time he moves.

One day, Theo is in a bookstore and he finds himself in the self-help section. He picks up a book on anger, and one of the suggestions catches his eye: "Keep an anger log." Theo isn't quite sure what that is, but he imagines that it's a sort of journal or diary in which he could write about his feelings of anger. He buys a notebook and, most nights, he writes a little bit before he goes to bed. He also finds himself writing in his journal whenever he feels bad about something and wishes he could talk to someone who would understand. Theo notices that, whether he thinks his anger is "justified" or not, he almost always feels better after he writes in his journal.

Mary Ellen is concerned. Her headaches have been getting worse. At the same time, she seems to be getting very angry about little things—Lissa being five minutes late for a shopping date, her mother making a dish that she knows that Mary Ellen doesn't like, her boyfriend forgetting something that she told him about her schedule. So far, she's been holding her anger in, because she knows that it doesn't fit the situation, plus she feels guilty and anxious every time she raises her voice or criticizes someone. But having all this anger inside her makes her nervous—what if she loses control and it gets out? Mary Ellen thinks of her anger as an ugly, poisonous volcano bubbling up inside her, threatening to explode.

Finally, Mary Ellen just can't take it any more. She feels ashamed of being angry—but she does bring herself to tell Lissa that some things her boyfriend does are really getting on her nerves. To her surprise, Lissa doesn't think any of it is such a big deal. She agrees with Mary Ellen that her boyfriend really is a great guy *but* that some of the things he does are really annoying. She doesn't seem to think Mary Ellen is a bad person for getting mad, and she doesn't seem worried about how Mary Ellen's boyfriend would feel if he found out she was angry. In fact, Lissa says, "He'll probably treat you better if you get on him once in a while." Mary Ellen feels relieved to have talked about at least part of her anger with someone who is so understanding.

Scott is starting to realize how much he doesn't like Julia's getting mad at him. When he tells this to Julia, she says, "But don't you get mad at me, too, sometimes?"

"Yes," says Scott, "but I try not to let you know, because I know how awful it is."

"Oh, come on!" says Julia. "First of all, I *always* know when you're mad at me—because you get so quiet. Second, I don't think it's so awful. I would a million times rather you tell me you're mad than have you try to *control* it the way you do."

"Well," says Scott, "what I want to know is, why do you *always* have to tell me when you're mad? If it's really important, OK, I understand, but sometimes it's just a little thing, and even when you say it doesn't mean very much—you just have to tell me about it. Couldn't you not tell me about it—sometimes?"

"Boy, the idea of *not* telling you *anything* just sounds so awful!" says Julia.

"Yeah, but why?" says Scott. "Besides, the idea of your being mad at me sounds awful to *me*."

"Why?" says Julia. "What's so awful about it?"

They look at each other in surprise. Each of them is so used to thinking that the other person has the problem. Neither has ever wondered before why he or she gets so upset about the other person's way of expressing anger.

Both of them have gotten really curious about why they have such strong fears about their anger. Scott decides that he will try to *visualize*—to picture and imagine—what he thinks would happen if he let his anger out. Julia decides that she will draw pictures of what she thinks might happen if she holds her anger in once in a while. They're both nervous—and curious—about what they might find out.

Tina is starting to get the feeling that she's just a fight looking to happen. She realizes that she often feels angry for no reason that she can see, so when arguments or disagreements come up, even about little things, she has all this anger to pour into them. She thinks of her anger as a rushing river, flooding through her, looking for a weak spot to break through the dam.

Tina decides she has to do something. She decides to try getting regular exercise—running twice a week and swimming on weekends—to blow off steam and make her feel less tense. She also decides to give up coffee and cola drinks, because she's heard that caffeine can also make people feel wound up. The exercise and the lack of caffeine help Tina to sleep better, so that she feels more rested. Tina still finds herself feeling angry more often than she would wish—but she doesn't feel as driven to get into fights, and she doesn't fly off the handle so easily.

Understanding Your Anger

The suggestions in the previous chapter were all based on one idea: In order to express your anger effectively, you have to understand what you're feeling and why. If you're talking about your friend's being five minutes late, but you're really thinking about the last four times she cancelled your plans, the expression of your anger is going to feel inappropriate, to both you and your friend. If you're talking about your friend's being five minutes late, but you're really feeling angry about the way your father always keeps you waiting, you're going to be even more puzzled about why you're giving your friend such a hard time for such a little thing.

So if you find that the techniques and suggestions for expressing anger don't work for you sometimes, you may really be angry about something else. In this chapter, we will talk more about understanding your anger—where it comes from, how it hides, and how to get in touch with it.

The Anger Cover-Up

Whether or not you're comfortable with anger has a lot to do with the lessons that your family taught you about that emotion. If your parents are comfortable with anger—in others and in themselves—it's likely that you will be too. In that case, you'll usually know why you're angry, and you'll find that you are angry some of the time.

Many parents, though, are not comfortable with anger— probably because they, too, were raised by parents who weren't comfortable with that emotion! In that case, they may pass on to their children messages that suggest or say explicitly that anger is a bad thing.

Believing that anger is bad can have many different results. Some of these include:

- **burying your anger**—trying to convince yourself and others that you are "never" angry
- **diverting your anger**—being afraid to be angry at whomever you're really mad at, so your anger comes out at a safer target
- **generalizing your anger**—being afraid to be angry at whomever you're really mad at, so your anger comes out all the time
- **disguising your anger**—feeling sad, depressed, hopeless, abandoned, lost, or lonely instead of feeling angry. Of course, sometimes people really do feel those emotions—but to people who believe that anger is bad, those emotions may feel safer than anger.

Ironically, the person who is always angry and the person who is "never" angry may both have the same problem— being afraid to know what they're really upset about. Both may also fear that their true anger will be destructive or dangerous to people they care about, which is why they have to either "bury" it or "spread it around." For both types of people, discovering what they're really feeling and becoming more comfortable with it will help to defuse their anger.

When You're Angry All the Time

The "Teenage Blues"

Many people find that the teenage years are an angry time. As we saw in Chapter 1, it's a time of separating from parents and family, which brings up anger in many people. It's also a time that most people find frustrating—too young to be out on your own, too old to accept your parents' ideas without question.

Your parents' expectations of you may also be changing, and your growing up may make *them* feel angry (along with proud, happy, excited, and other positive feelings). They, too, may be frustrated that you're no longer their little baby, whom they know how to take care of; instead, your new maturity means that they have to change their ideas about what you need and what their responsibilities are. Many people find change upsetting or scary, and many people handle those feelings by getting angry.

So if you go through periods of unexplained anger, some of what may be bothering you is just "the teenage blues"— the normal frustrations of trying to figure out your new values and abilities as you are growing up. If, however, your anger is making you feel profoundly unhappy, if you're scared or anxious about what your anger seems to be leading to, or if you feel that your anger is getting in the way of your relationships with friends, family, dating partners, or people at school, then you may want to look into your anger more closely.

Being Aware of What You Feel

The first step toward understanding your anger is to get in touch with it. Many people who are "always" angry don't quite realize that that is what they're feeling. They have different words for their feelings: disturbed, upset, bothered, annoyed, irritated, not pleased, a little out of it. They may also frequently feel anxious, guilty, depressed, or hopeless—which are ways that people often react to feelings of anger that they think they "shouldn't" have.

Here are some clues to figuring out whether you are very frequently angry:*

- Do you complain a lot about little things—a person's ugly hairstyle, a missing textbook, a bad driver?
- Do you frequently feel critical and annoyed with other people's stupidity, bad fashion habits, or inconsiderate ways?
- Do you find yourself frequently disagreeing with friends, teachers, parents, or other family members, especially about things that don't directly affect your life—the "gross" foods they like to eat, the stupid movies they enjoy, the awful political ideas they hold?
- Do you find yourself mocking people or making jokes that others find insulting (even if you thought you only intended to be funny)?
- Do you often get into arguments with strangers—people standing in line with you, other drivers, store clerks?
- Do you often get into arguments with the person you're dating, with your best friend, or with other people you see regularly?
- Does your anger frequently catch you off guard, so that you find yourself going very quickly from feeling calm and relaxed to feeling furious or enraged?

---

*This list has been adapted from material found in Williams's *Anger Kills* and Theodore Isaac Rubin's *The Angry Book*.

- Are you cynical about most people and organizations, feeling that "Most people don't mean what they say," or "You can't trust most grown-ups," or "It's surprising how many people are just phonies"?
- Do you feel that most people just don't come up to your standards?
- Do you feel that you yourself usually don't come up to your own standards?
- Do you often feel depressed, anxious, hopeless, or guilty?

Again, feeling any of these ways *some* of the time is a normal part of life—and especially, a normal part of most people's teenage years. Becoming disillusioned with the world around you, especially with the grown-ups in it, is part of growing up and developing your own ideas about how things should be. But if most of the items on this checklist apply to you most of the time, you may be angrier than you realize. Your anger may be more than the daily frustrations of being a teenager; it may be giving you a signal that a person or situation in your life is bothering you a great deal.

Identifying the Sources of Your Feelings

If you do feel concerned about your anger, the first step is to get in touch with what's really bothering you. Often, people need help to do this, possibly talking to a counselor or a therapist. (For more about getting help, see Chapter 6.) There are also some steps you can take on your own:

- **Write about your feelings.** Some people find it helpful to write something in a journal or diary every night. Other people like to pick up their journals whenever the spirit moves them. Still other people turn to their diaries whenever they find themselves feeling angry. In any case, you can "tell" your most private thoughts to a journal, trying out different statements or exploring ideas that you would never share with anyone else.

- **Keep an anger log.** Theo wasn't quite clear about how an anger log differed from a journal, but it's very simple. Every time you find yourself getting angry, you can use an anger log to jot down why. You can also note some other facts about your anger in your log. When Theo finally found out what an anger log was, he started keeping one in addition to a journal. Here's a sample entry from his log. Note the different questions he answers about each time he feels angry, as well as the different answers that he found. (The questions are in italic type, and Theo's answers are in regular type.)

Time and Date: 10 o'clock, Saturday, April 15th
What happened? Mom said I had to baby-sit
On a scale of 1 to 10, how angry was I?: 9
How did I express it? told Mom I was mad, yelled at her
How long did my anger last? all day and for a couple of hours after I went to bed
Any problems with my anger? I couldn't sleep

Time and Date: noon, Saturday, April 15th
What happened? Keesha started crying
On a scale of 1 to 10, how angry was I? 2
How did I express it? did nothing
How long did my anger last? 15 minutes
Any problems with my anger? my stomach hurt a little

After you've been keeping your anger log for two weeks or so, you might read it over and see whether you can find any patterns. What kinds of things make you angry most often? How do you usually handle them? Do any particular people keep popping up? Is there any type of treatment that you're especially upset about? Reading over your log, what's your first reaction? Your second reaction?

It's helpful to write about your feelings on a separate page in your anger log. See what discoveries you make! If you find it helpful, you might want to continue keeping your log, checking back again in another two weeks. Does your log give you any ideas for changes you want to make in your life, new ways for handling your anger, or issues that you want to discuss with a particular person?*

- **Talk to a friend.** A sympathetic friend who will accept your anger and respond to you honestly can often help you identify what's really going on with you. Sometimes, all a friend has to do is listen, letting you talk through your thoughts and feelings, allowing you to try out saying a variety of different things until you hear what sounds right to you. Sometimes a friend can ask questions or point out things that will help you see issues more clearly.

- **Use your dreams.** Our dreams often reveal our innermost thoughts and feelings. Usually, they do so in a mysterious language of images and symbols, but with patience and practice, you can interpret the messages you are trying to give yourself. It's usually helpful to keep a dream journal by your bed, and to write down a description of your dreams first thing every morning. (If you're a visual person, you might draw pictures of the images in your dream instead.) Even if you usually don't remember your dreams, you'd be surprised how deciding to write them down will help you to remember them. If writing down a dream gives you any ideas about things that are of concern in your life, jot down those thoughts too. Otherwise, just write down your dreams. After you've done that for a couple of weeks, read back over what you've written. Then, on a separate sheet of paper, write the question "Why am I angry?" and commit yourself to writing without stopping for at least five minutes. Just write down anything that comes to mind. Don't worry about using complete sentences, about making sense, or about anything except keeping your pen or pencil moving.

---

* A discussion of "Anger Diaries" can be found in Hankins's *Prescription for Anger;* Albert Ellis also writes about keeping written records in *Anger: How to Live With and Without It.*

When you've finished writing, take a deep breath. What did you discover? How are you feeling? Upset? Relieved? Worried? Nervous? Excited? Calm? You might make one or two more notes to record that. Then go back to writing down your dreams for another two weeks before you repeat this process again. Even if you don't come up with any logical answers, you may find that just paying attention to your dreams in this way helps you feel more in touch with your emotions or brings you some kind of relief from the parts of your anger that you've found troubling.

When You're "Never" Angry

Being "Nice" All the Time

Are you someone who is never angry? Of course, that might really be the way you feel—but it may also be that your anger is coming out in other ways. Do any of the following questions ring any bells with you?*

- Do you find yourself bothered a lot by little things?
- Have you been avoiding friends whom you once liked— "for no good reason"?
- Do you have a lot of accidents, ones that either hurt you or cause problems for other people?
- Are you frequently late?
- Do you have trouble falling asleep?
- Do you have trouble sleeping all the way through the night or sleeping until a reasonable time in the morning?
- Do you find yourself taking reckless chances, such as driving too fast or experimenting with dangerous drugs?
- Do you frequently forget things?

---

*Sources for these questions include Rubin's *The Angry Book* and the Hankins's *Prescription for Anger*.

- Do you often make mistakes that end up causing a great deal of difficulty to yourself or others? (Everybody makes mistakes sometimes! We're talking about a pattern that puzzles or upsets you.)
- Do you find yourself worrying a lot about whether other people are hurt or upset?
- Do you frequently feel guilty—whether for a "good reason," a bad reason, or no reason?
- Are you or the people around you concerned that you're working too hard or doing too much? Are you the kind of person who never has a free minute?
- Do you have problems with overeating or undereating?
- Do you feel compelled to drink or to use drugs regularly?
- Do you frequently get sick, especially with "little" problems such as headaches, sore throats, colds, stomachaches, or backaches?
- Do you find yourself losing interest in the romantic side of things with a boyfriend or girlfriend, or does your interest stop and start in ways that you don't understand?
- Do you feel depressed, hopeless, or without energy?

Of course, anyone might say yes to one or two of those questions at some point, and a problem with any of them doesn't necessarily mean you have a problem with anger. But buried anger usually does come out, often in the ways suggested by the checklist. If you find yourself answering "yes" to several of the questions, or if you find yourself feeling anxious or upset just thinking about them, you may be burying your anger.

Passive-Aggressive Behavior

Psychologists have a word for subtle expressions of angry behavior—they call them "passive-aggressive." This means that a person is behaving aggressively, or hurtfully, but in a way that disguises his or her true intention—from himself/herself as well as from others.

As she talked things over with Lissa, Mary Ellen started to realize that her mother, who was also "never" angry, was actually very passive-aggressive. For example, once Mary Ellen's mother asked Mary Ellen to baby-sit her younger brothers and sisters for a whole weekend while her parents took a short vacation. Mary Ellen said, "Gee, Mom, I'm really busy this weekend. I'd have to cancel my date with my boyfriend, and Lissa and I were going shopping. Couldn't you pick another time?"

"Oh, that's all right," said Mary Ellen's mother. "Of course, your father hasn't been feeling well lately, and we thought that it would do him good to get away, but it probably won't make that much difference if he waits for a while. Of course, then we won't be able to get the discount at the hotel— they're only offering that this weekend. But that doesn't matter. You run along and have fun."

Mary Ellen finds herself feeling guilty. She doesn't want to damage her father's health, and she doesn't want to cost her parents money by making them miss the discount. So she swallows her feelings and says, "Never mind, Mom, I'd be glad to baby- sit."

"Oh, would you?" says her mother. "That's so nice of you! You're just the sweetest daughter!"

As she talks about this incident with Lissa, Mary Ellen comes to see that her mother wasn't really being honest. After all, she could have just come straight out and said, "Mary Ellen, you don't have a choice. Your father and I need you to baby-sit this weekend. I'm sorry you have to cancel your plans, but we are your parents, and this weekend, we come first."

Mary Ellen might or might not have liked hearing her mother tell her to baby-sit. She might even have thought it was unfair or wrong. At least, though, her mother would have been open about what she was doing—putting her own needs and wishes first, and insisting that Mary Ellen put herself second. Since her mother would have been clear about what she was doing, Mary Ellen might have been able to understand why she herself felt angry.

Instead, Mary Ellen's mother pretends to accept Mary Ellen's answer—and then does everything she can to make Mary Ellen feel guilty about it. Trying to make Mary Ellen feel bad so she'll change her mind is really a hurtful or aggressive thing to do. But instead of saying hurtful things straight out ("You're a bad daughter!"), Mary Ellen's mother hides the fact that she's being hurtful ("Of course, your father hasn't been feeling well lately"). This makes it much harder for Mary Ellen to get angry—how can she get angry at something that her mother isn't even admitting that she's doing?

Here are some other examples of passive-aggressive behavior. All of them are ways in which people hurt, get back at, or control someone without admitting that they're doing so.

*Examples of Passive-Aggressive Behavior**

- forgetting what someone has told you
- forgetting to do something that you promised to do, thereby causing trouble for someone else
- accidentally ruining someone's property
- accidentally bumping into someone or otherwise hurting him or her
- making jokes that hurt people's feelings
- teasing—and saying "I'm only joking!" when the person gets upset
- asking "innocent" questions that hurt people's feelings (for example, "Have you gained weight? I just wondered," or "Where's your boyfriend tonight?")
- inducing guilt
- pouting
- being quiet

---

*Sources for this list include Rubin's *The Angry Book* and Hankins's *Prescription for Anger.*

- reading or watching television while someone is trying to talk to you
- acting confused, not understanding an explanation or instructions, making someone repeat himself or herself a lot
- dawdling
- being late
- putting things off
- not hearing someone who's talking to you
- insisting that you're not angry when you are
- doing better than someone else with the intention of showing the other person up
- condescending to or patronizing another person, acting superior or pitying
- agreeing with everything someone says when you don't really mean it
- being sarcastic or pessimistic, so that everything the other person says seems useless or silly
- being tired—especially if it means you're too tired to do something that someone else wants to do, or if it means you can't enjoy a special time with another person
- getting sick—especially if it affects plans you've already made
- suddenly losing interest in being romantic with a boy-friend or girlfriend, especially when he or she is expecting a romantic time

Is every single item on that list passive-aggressive all the time? Of course not. Sometimes people really don't feel like being romantic, or do feel like reading, or just get tired, or really are confused. What makes an action passive-aggressive is the intention behind it. If it's done to cause another person pain, to get revenge for something that the person did, or to control the other person and manipulate his or her behavior, then the action is passive-aggressive.

How can you tell when another person is being passive-aggressive, or when you are yourself? There are no surefire rules; you'll just have to trust your instincts. Here are some clues, however, that might help you sharpen your instincts as you think about this issue:

- **Is there a regular pattern to the behavior?** Do you find yourself getting tired every time you have to do something you really don't want to do?
- **What effect did the behavior have on the other people in the situation?** Did your little sister get furious after you were "only joking" about her "ugly hairdo"?
- **Was there anything in the situation that might have made someone angry?** Did you "just not feel like talking" after your boyfriend broke a date?

Sometimes passive-aggressive behavior is an expression of anger. Sometimes it's a way to control or manipulate others. Either way, passive-aggressive people often make *other* people angry, since no one likes to be hurt, controlled, or manipulated.

If a family's anger style is passive-aggressive, or if one family member has this style, it can often be very difficult for the children to feel comfortable with their own anger. Sometimes this is because the passive-aggressive parent seems to be always nice, never angry (although many people who yell and scream or who otherwise openly express anger may also act in passive-aggressive ways). If a parent seems never to be angry, his or her child is likely to feel that there's something wrong with that emotion. The child doesn't realize that the parent *is* angry and is simply burying the anger. So the child feels guilty when he or she discovers his or her own anger.

Often, too, passive-aggressive people are very difficult to get angry at. That's because they never admit—perhaps not even to themselves—what they are doing. When Scott gives Julia the silent treatment, for example, she gets madder and madder—but he can calmly say, "What's the big deal? I'm not doing anything!" Or when Julia teases Scott and he gets mad, she can say, "Why are you so sensitive? I was only joking!" This denial makes it far more difficult to communicate honestly and openly.

Remember, passive-aggressive behavior doesn't tell us anything about why a person is angry, or whether the anger is "justified," or in what other ways a person might legitimately express his or her anger. Scott might have good reason to be mad at Julia for teasing him in front of their friends; Julia might have every right to resent getting the silent treatment from her boyfriend. As long as they are both burying their anger in passive-aggressive behavior, though, it will be a lot harder for them to see what's really happening—and their painful fights are likely to continue.

Likewise, a person might do something that makes another person angry and still not be passive-aggressive. If Mary Ellen's mother had insisted that her daughter baby-sit, Mary Ellen might have felt angry or upset. But her mother's *intention* would not have been to hurt Mary Ellen; her intention would have been to take a short vacation. Sometimes people do feel hurt or angry by the things we do, but that's quite different from deliberately trying to make them feel bad so we can get them to do what we want.

Of course, the upsetting thing about passive-aggressive behavior is that it's often more hurtful than a direct expression of one's anger or of one's wishes might be. Telling your friend, "I don't want to see that movie!" might be easier on both of you than your getting a headache just as the credits are rolling, thereby ruining the rest of the evening for you both. Hearing directly that your mother wants you to do something unpleasant might be easier—even if it's annoying—than feeling guilty about what a bad son or daughter you are.

What's So Scary About Getting Angry?

People who bury their anger often feel frightened of that emotion. Consciously or without realizing it, they may feel that one or more of the following statements is true:

- **Feeling angry will hurt or even kill someone they love.** This belief is especially common among people who have experienced a death in their families. Even people who have not had a loved one die, however, often have strong fears about the effects of their anger.
- **Feeling angry will drive a loved one away.** Children of divorced parents may be especially prone to believe this. They may feel that their anger (or other "bad" things about them) drove one of their parents away. Or they may feel that the anger of one of their parents drove the other parent away, and fear their own anger accordingly.
- **Feeling angry will take away their power.** Some people experience their anger as out of their control. When they feel angry, they feel like a child having a tantrum—and they feel ashamed of not being able to control themselves better.
- **Feeling angry will give them too much power.** People who never or rarely express their anger directly may have fantasies about being able to get anything they want—just by being angry. They may feel guilty about having that kind of power, at the same time that they secretly believe that they *could* have it.

Although none of those beliefs is true, all of them can carry a lot of power in our minds, especially if they're hidden. If you feel that you're scared of or uncomfortable about anger but don't quite know why, you might use one of the techniques we've already discussed to learn more about yourself—writing in a journal, talking to a friend, recording your dreams and asking yourself "What happens if I get angry?" You might also use *visualization* to find out more about what you feel.

Using Visualization
Visualization is a technique that can be used for many purposes. Here, we're suggesting a way of using it to get in touch with your feelings.

Find a safe, private place to do this exercise. Make sure you won't be interrupted and that you're comfortable. You might want to put on some soothing music or do anything else that you find relaxing before you start. (It's best not to try this after drinking or taking drugs, however—the exercise requires a clear head.)

Close your eyes and picture a competely safe, pleasant place. Picture as many details as you can—what it looks like, what smells you notice, whether it's warm or cold, what sounds you hear. After about five minutes, picture yourself moving away from this safe place into another location, where you meet someone with whom you get angry. See as many details as you can of the person with whom you're angry. (If you're nervous about doing this exercise thinking of a real person, you might picture getting angry at someone you don't know, such as a clerk in a store.) Picture the incident that's making you mad. (Again, you might picture an imaginary incident, such as a clerk saying something insulting to you, or a stranger pushing you hard as you're crossing the street.)

In the incident that you're picturing, allow yourself to get mad. What happens? It may make you uncomfortable to imagine yourself getting mad, but stay with it as long as you can. Remind yourself that any time you like, you can go back to the safe place you pictured before.

When you've learned all you can by observing yourself in the angry situation, take yourself back to that safe place and stay there for another minute or two, until you feel relaxed and calm again. Then open your eyes and remember what you visualized.

Many people find it helpful to write about or draw what they saw. After doing so, you might write "What happens when I get angry?" at the top of a separate page, and then ask yourself to write without stopping for five minutes, just to see what you say. What did you learn?

Don't forget that what you visualized expresses your *thoughts* about being angry, not what would actually happen. If you pictured your anger as a huge flame burning everything up, that tells you what you're worried about or perhaps what you *wish* you could do—but it does not tell you what would actually happen. If you pictured beating someone up, or the other person collapsing, or some other painful or disastrous incident, you have learned something about your ideas about anger—but you have not found out anything about what *really* happens when you get angry. *That* you can learn only from real life, not from visualization!

Aggressive or Assertive?

People who bury anger sometimes have difficulty understanding the difference between *aggressive* and *assertive*. Aggressive behavior is intended to hurt or control others. Assertive behavior is intended to set limits and express one's own feelings. It's possible for two assertive people to "agree to disagree," to reach a compromise, or to work out their differences, because both of them want a situation where everybody wins. An aggressive person, on the other hand, may feel that he or she has not really "won" unless somebody else loses.

Of course, sometimes people who bury anger have trouble both with assertion and with aggression. They may have somehow gotten the message that they have no rights, that they must always put others first, or that any kind of self-protection makes them selfish. Figuring out what you owe to others, what you're willing to sacrifice for them, and what constitutes taking care of yourself, is a tricky problem. It often takes years to figure this out—and you're probably just beginning! Still, it's helpful to remember that there can be a difference between taking care of yourself and hurting another person. A quotation from an ancient Jewish rabbi, Rabbi Hillel, sums up the need for balancing self-protection with concern for others:

> If I am not for myself, who will be for me?
> If I am only for myself, what am I?
> And if not now, when?

Releasing Your Anger

Once you know that you're angry and why you're angry, what do you do then? In some cases, of course, the best answer is to take action. You might turn to Chapter 3 for some suggestions on how to express your anger. You might need to make some changes in your life, now that you've become aware of problems or people that are making you angry. You might decide that you need a counselor's help and support, or that you need some other kind of help (if so, see Chapters 6 and 7).

You may also decide that you need to let go of some of your anger, especially if you find that you're angry about things that have happened in the past or about situations that you can't control. Letting go of your anger doesn't mean burying it, controlling it, or deciding that it wasn't really justified. Letting go of your anger means feeling the feeling, fully and completely—and then allowing yourself to move on.

Forgiving, Absolving, and Letting Go

Some people talk about letting go of anger as "forgiving." They suggest that until you forgive the people who have hurt you, you'll stay involved with those people. In a sense, your anger is keeping those people alive and present in your memory, even if you no longer know them.

We agree that anger tends to keep you involved with the people or situations that you're angry at. And we agree that forgiving others—and yourself—is an important part of moving on. We urge you, though, to make sure you've had a chance to feel all your feelings, the angry ones as well as the loving ones, before you move on to forgiveness.

We also want to remind you that forgiving someone is not the same as *absolving* them. To absolve someone is to say that he or she has not really done anything wrong or to say that he or she has made full amends for the wrong. To forgive someone is only to say that *you* are no longer going to remain concerned with that person's wrongdoing.

Sometimes forgiveness can include absolution. Perhaps you understand that the person who hurt you didn't do so intentionally, or was acting under extenuating circumstances, or deserves your sympathy in some other way. Perhaps the person has apologized, or tried to make it up to you, and you feel satisfied with his or her response.

But what if you feel that the person acted badly or unfairly and that there's really no excuse for that behavior? What if you believe that the person acted badly but the person does not agree? What if the person seems to have apologized, but you don't feel that he or she is really sincere or that his or her actions reflect true understanding of what went wrong? Or perhaps you feel that what the person did was so bad that no explanation really matters and no apology is possible. Can you still forgive the person?

We believe that you can. In this sense, forgiving a person is like forgiving a debt. Being angry with someone is like saying that he or she owes you something—your anger suggests that the person should make up for the bad thing he or she did. Forgiving someone might be like saying, "I don't expect to collect that debt any more. I'm going to let that go." The person may still be "bad" for owing you, but you're not concerned with him or her any more. You've let go of your anger and moved on to other things.

Forgiving in that sense would also allow you to protect yourself from someone who you feel might hurt you badly again. Forgiving doesn't have to mean wiping the slate clean and starting over—it only means that you're no longer interested in feeling angry about something that is now over and can't be changed.

Because anger is such an uncomfortable emotion for so many people, people often want to move very quickly to forgiveness or "getting past" their anger. If you don't get in touch with your anger, though, forgiveness isn't really possible. The anger will still be there, and it will come out in some other way—perhaps against another person, perhaps against yourself. Only after you've "had" your anger can you let it go.

Ways to Release Your Anger

If you're ready to let go of your anger, what can you do? Many of the suggestions we've made for getting in touch with your anger can also be used to help you release it. Here are several ideas for releasing all types of anger, from minor irritation to genuine rage, from anger at trivial incidents to anger at serious abuse or betrayal.

Write or draw a picture about your feelings. Keeping a journal and expressing your feelings can be very helpful in working through anger. According to studies whose results were published in 1987 and 1988 by James W. Pennebaker (described in Carol Tavris's *Anger: The Misunderstood Emotion*), writing about traumatic experiences helped people cope with them better. Pennebaker said that writing about difficult or painful experiences was very important because thoughts about traumatic events tended to be *obsessive*—the person returned to thinking about the incident over and over again. Such thoughts also tend to be poorly organized and incomplete.

In other words, a person who thought obsessively about a wrong done to him or her simply went back over the same ground again and again. That obsessive person didn't really learn anything from the experience and continued to feel angry and upset by it. A person who wrote about his or her experience, however, tended to gain insight from organizing the thoughts and describing the experience. This insight was crucial to people's being able to reinterpret an upsetting incident—and then to put it behind them.

Talk to a friend. Talking to a friend can work in the same way as writing in a journal—you have the chance to move forward, coming to new insights and new ways of seeing your experience. These new thoughts can allow you to move on to other feelings: acceptance instead of resentment, forgiveness instead of anger. You may find new ways to accept yourself, as well, forgiving yourself for your own mistakes, weaknesses, and vulnerabilities.

However, if talking with a friend becomes obsessive—going over the same ground again and again—it actually helps keep you angry. Repeating an angry story or reiterating the same old complaints are almost like *rehearsing* your anger—keeping it alive and fresh and actually preventing you from moving on. A little "venting" can be good for a while—but if it goes on for too long or is repeated too frequently, it may keep you angry rather than helping you to release your anger.

Turn your anger into art. Write a short story about the person or incident that made you angry. Put your angry feelings into a poem, a piece of music, a sculpture, or a collage. Tell the world what *really* happened, express the pain you felt, show the villainous face of the person who hurt you. Often, what keeps us angry is being deprived of the space or the strength to assert our own feelings, our own vision of what went on. Using art to present your vision may bring you a sense of release—as well as giving others a chance to learn from your experience!

Take care of yourself physically. As Tina found, getting vigorous exercise and sufficient sleep helped relieve a lot of the tension that was feeding her anger. Likewise, cutting out caffeine (found in coffee, tea, and cola drinks), nicotine, and other types of drugs has a naturally calming effect. Cutting out alcohol—or cutting back to a drink or two once a week—can also help your outlook, since alcohol puts such a strain on your system. A diet rich in calcium (found in dairy products and green leafy vegetables) and vitamin B (found in whole grains, such as brown rice or whole wheat—and in vitamin supplements) helps your body manage anger better.

If improving your physical condition doesn't solve all the problems you have with anger, you may need to do some further exploring. Even so, giving your body the gift of health is a great resource that can help you along your emotional journey.

Use fantasy. Are you furious with someone who has done you wrong? Imagine the punishment you would like to mete out. Or imagine the person feeling sorry and ashamed. Give yourself the revenge or the reconciliation in fantasy that you are about to give up hoping for in reality. You may want simply to imagine this fantastic scene, or you might prefer to write it down. Some people enjoy sharing their fantasies with a friend—especially their fantasies of revenge! (Be sure to pick a friend who is comfortable with anger, though, so he or she can support you in your wishes without worrying that you're really planning to retaliate.)

Develop a ritual. Are you having trouble letting go of a person or a relationship? Perhaps you need a ritual to mark an ending. Or perhaps you'd like to forgive someone whom you still want in your life, and you'd like a ritual to help you release the anger that is coming between you.

What might your ritual look like? That's up to you! You're looking for whatever will help you acknowledge and then release your anger. Here are a few suggestions that might help you to develop rituals of your own:

- Writing down your angry thoughts on scraps of paper and then burning them.
- Making a package of things or pictures associated with a person or a painful time, and then putting the package away, burying it, or giving it away.
- Writing a person or a group of people a letter, telling them your grievances, and then burning, burying, or putting

away the letter. (*Don't* send it—unless you're prepared to deal with the response! In that case, you would not have been completing a ritual to let go of anger, but rather taking further action.)

- Drawing a picture that expresses saying goodbye to the person, place, or time that has caused you pain. Show yourself walking away, flying high over the scene, or floating on a boat far beyond the people on shore.

Use humor. The great thing about seeing the funny side of things is that it means you're seeing *another* side. As we've seen, releasing your anger is based on moving on to a new perspective. One of the best ways of getting a new perspective is through laughter—especially laughter at yourself! Writer and critic Norman Cousins once claimed that laughter helped him cure himself of a debilitating disease. Laughter can truly be a healing force!

Ways That Probably Won't Help You Release Your Anger

Although you are the only one who can decide how to release your anger, here are a few techniques that probably *won't* help:

- **Venting.** There's a popular myth that if you "get your anger out" it won't bother you anymore. Yelling at someone, or yelling at the person as though he or she were there, will not necessarily help you release your anger, however. Studies cited by Carol Tavris in *Anger: The Misunderstood Emotion* show that blasting someone with your anger doesn't necessarily make you feel less angry—it can sometimes make you feel more angry, or angry for a longer time. If, in your venting, you allow yourself to say cruel or hurtful things, you may provoke the other person to revenge or retaliation, as well as making yourself feel guilty, ashamed, or depressed about your own behavior.

- **Hitting.** Both actually hitting another person and punching a pillow or a punching bag can also make you feel more angry, rather than less. As Tavris says, aggression tends to lead to more aggression. Putting your anger into physical aggression—even against a pillow—seems to give your body the message that it really *is* in danger and needs to turn on the "fight or flight" hormones, rather than helping you to calm down.
- **Using liquor, drugs, or food to calm yourself down.** Using liquor, drugs, or food to "stuff" or "swallow" your anger may help you feel temporarily more calm. But don't confuse that with releasing your anger. These physical substances may help you *bury* your anger, but they are unlikely to help you feel it, resolve it, and let it go. (If you're concerned about ways that you use drugs, alcohol, or food, see Chapters 6 and 7.)

Coming to Terms with Anger

Learning how to find, feel, act on, and then release your anger is no easy task! It often takes people years to get to know themselves, and even longer to get comfortable with themselves. But making this journey of self-discovery is one of the most challenging and rewarding parts of becoming an adult. Starting to explore these issues now will continue to pay off for the rest of your life.

5

Coping with Someone Else's Anger

Theo's friend Laurence has a real problem. Laurence's father drinks a lot, and when he gets drunk, he comes home and yells at his wife, at Laurence, and at the rest of the kids. Laurence is really angry with his father, all the time. Sometimes when his father is drunk, Laurence just tries to stay out of his way; sometimes he yells back, but that just seems to make things worse. In fact, Laurence's mother has started saying that *he* is the reason that his father drinks—if he would just behave better, his father wouldn't feel so pressured, and even if he did drink, he wouldn't yell so much. Being blamed for his father's problem makes Laurence feel even angrier—and he also secretly wonders whether his mother isn't right.

Theo tells his friend about his anger log, and Laurence gives it a try. It helps some, but not enough. "I don't know, Theo," Laurence says one day. "I'm not sure I can take it any more." Theo feels terrible. Isn't there some way his friend can get help?

If you asked Mary Ellen whether she was having trouble with anyone else's anger, she'd probably say, "Oh, no, not at all." But she's been noticing that she's becoming more and more frustrated with her mother lately—much as she tries to stay nice and cheerful—and Lissa suggests that Mary Ellen may be having trouble because of the way Mary Ellen's mother takes her anger out on Mary Ellen.

At first, Mary Ellen has no idea what Lissa is talking about. But slowly she starts to realize that the things her mother says aren't always very nice—even though her mother always says them with a big smile. When Mary Ellen came down to breakfast one day, feeling under the weather, her mother said cheerfully, "Well, don't you look like something the cat dragged in!" Her mother's remark made Mary Ellen feel terrible. But when Mary Ellen tried to laugh it off, saying, "Oh, shoot, I wanted to look nice for my speech in civics class today," her mother followed up her remark with another zinger: "Well, too bad for you, Mary Ellen, because let's face it, this is *not* one of your better days, sweetheart!"

Another day, Mary Ellen came home feeling upset about her fight with Judith. "Now is that the kind of face I like to see on my girl?" her mother said as soon as Mary Ellen walked into the house. "Let me see a smile!" Mary Ellen tried to smile, but her heart wasn't in it. "Come on, smile!" her mother insisted. "You're so much prettier when you smile." Mary Ellen felt really bad. Not only was she already down about her fight with Judith, but now she seemed to be upsetting her mother, too, by not smiling.

When she talks about it with Lissa, Lissa says, "But Mary Ellen! Who wants to hear that they look like something the cat dragged in? What a terrible thing for your mother to say! And why *should* you smile when you're feeling down? Making you smile when you don't feel like it is *mean*! Maybe she's not doing it on purpose, but your mother is taking her stuff out on you."

Scott and Julia also have a friend they're concerned about—Valerie. Valerie's mother has a terrible temper, and when she gets really mad, she hits Valerie. Mostly, Valerie just has a few bruises to show for it, but Scott and Julia are worried that someday, it may get worse. Valerie insists that nothing bad is going on—her mother is just very strict. "When Mom was growing up, her grandmother used to give her a whipping when she was bad. She says it worked for her, so it will work for me," Valerie explains.

"I don't know," Julia says. "I don't think it's fair for her to hurt you that way."

"Well, if I've been bad . . ." Valerie says.

"Valerie, you're a great person," says Scott. "Nothing you do could be that bad."

Scott and Julia want Valerie to tell someone about what's happening to her—someone who could possibly help her family and get her mother to stop hitting her. But Valerie is scared. If her mother was mad at her before, she's going to be really mad if she finds out Valerie has been complaining about her. Plus, Valerie feels guilty. She thinks that talking about her problem to another grown-up is like betraying her family. Besides, what would happen? Would her mother go to jail? Would they take Valerie away from her? Valerie certainly doesn't want any of that to happen.

Tina *knows* she has a problem with her father's anger. She doesn't so much mind the open fighting, where she gets to say what she thinks and he says what he thinks. What she minds is the insulting things he says about her when they're *not* having a big fight. Her father has this way of saying angry, insulting things in a kind of offhand tone, which hurts Tina's feelings really badly, even though she doesn't like to admit it, even to herself. When Tina came home with a C in biology, for example, her father just sighed disgustedly and said, "Well, what do you expect from someone like her?" Or when Tina's father did let her go to Marisol's party, and Tina came home right on time as she promised, her father shrugged and said, "For once, you did the right thing—I can hardly believe it!" Tina gets the feeling that her father is always disgusted with her, and that whatever she does will never be good enough for him.

When You're the Target of Someone Else's Anger

What if your "anger problem" is really a problem with somebody else's anger? You may not be able to control the other person's choices about how to express his or her anger, but you can certainly set limits and make clear how you expect to be treated.

Angry people often believe that they are somehow out of control or not responsible when they get angry. They may experience their anger as a force that drives them to yell, to insult others, or even to commit physical violence. After their temper has passed, they may feel sorry for what they did or said while "under the influence" of anger. If they were drunk or high while they were angry, they may be even more insistent that the drugs or liquor were responsible for their anger, not them.

In fact, none of this is true. While we may not be able to control *feeling* angry, all of us have choices about what we *do* while we are angry. Likewise, a person who is drunk or high is still responsible for his or her actions. He or she can choose not to use drugs or alcohol, or can decide to stay away from family members or from people in general while drunk or high. You have a right to expect the people in your life to express their anger appropriately, no matter what the circumstances. You have a right to set limits with people and to demand decent treatment.

Likewise, angry people may express their anger in subtle ways. As we discussed in Chapter 4, this may take the form of *passive-aggressive* anger—anger in which the angry person rather passively pretends not to be doing anything, even though his or her behavior is actually quite aggressive, or attacking.

Mary Ellen's mother may be considered passive-aggressive. Even though she seems to be smiling, cheerful, and friendly, she is acting quite aggressively, in one case insulting Mary Ellen ("You look like something the cat dragged in!"); in another case insisting that Mary Ellen do what her mother wants, no matter how Mary Ellen feels about it ("Smile!").

Tina's father may also be considered passive-aggressive, even though he also expresses his anger more openly, in outright fights with Tina. When he is not actually fighting with her, however, he is still treating her in an angry way. His insulting remarks express that he is angry with her, even if Tina can't always figure out what she's done wrong (Is he mad because she got a low grade, or because he thinks she's really stupid? Is he angry because sometimes she comes home late, or because this time she came home on time?).

Both Tina's father and Mary Ellen's mother treat their children in confusing and frustrating ways. If they were direct and honest about their anger, their children might be unhappy, but at least they'd know where they stood. Since their anger comes out in insults, unreasonable requests, and expressions of disappointment, their children can't figure out who's really responsible for the problem or what they— Tina and Mary Ellen—can do about it.

Setting Limits

Recall the distinction we made in Chapter 4 between being *aggressive* and being *assertive*. An aggressive person tries to control or dominate others, whether through anger or through some other means. An assertive person, on the other hand, is not interested in changing other people's behavior, but rather in making sure that he or she is treated well. Being assertive means saying how unpleasant behavior is affecting you and asking for what you want.

Here are some suggestions for things that assertive people can say to angry, aggressive people to set limits with them:

- "Please don't yell at me. I can hear you better when you speak in a normal voice."
- "That hurt my feelings. I don't want to be talked to that way."
- "I don't want to talk to you while you're this angry. When you're calmer, then we'll talk."
- "I don't want to talk to you while you're drunk (or high). When you're sober (or straight), then we'll talk."

If a person is frequently angry or abusive and makes you the target of that rage, you might want to decide on what kind of relationship you want with that person. You may feel that such a person is not a good friend or dating partner for you. If the person is a member of your family, you can choose to avoid the person as much as possible, to stand up to him or her when you have no choice, and possibly to ask another adult to intervene and help the difficult person learn to treat you better.

What about setting limits with a person who is treating you in a passive-aggressive way? That can be harder, because in addition to doing the work of setting the limits, you also have to figure out by yourself what the problem is. Still, once you realize what's going on, you *can* set limits on this kind of behavior, as well. The trick is to keep your eye on your goal—to make the behavior stop. You probably won't be able to make the other person aware of what he or she is doing, nor get the person to agree that he or she is doing something wrong. But you *may* be able to insist that the person stop—or at least express your own feelings about what the person is doing, whether he or she stops or not.

Here are some suggestions for things that assertive people can say to set limits with passive-aggressive people:

- "That really hurt my feelings."
- "Please don't say anything to me about how I look."
- "I don't agree."
- "Sometime I'd like to hear about the things I do right, and not just the things I do wrong."
- "OK, I've heard your opinion. I don't need to hear it again."
- "I'm feeling attacked, and I don't like it."
- "I don't want to hear this."
- "Stop. Just stop."
- "Cut it out."

(The last two suggestions may be especially effective, because the passive-aggressive person usually knows, somewhere deep down, that he or she *is* attacking or provoking you. You can tell the person to stop without insisting that he or she acknowledge what's been going on.)

How can you tell whether a person's seemingly attacking behavior is an accident or is really passive-aggressive—that is, intended to hurt you? You can't always be sure, but you can often tell by the way the person responds. If you say, calmly and quietly, "That hurts my feelings," or "Please stop," and the other person shows concern (even if they stick to their guns about the point they're making or the request they have), then they probably did not intend to attack or hurt you. If your expression of hurt feelings or your assertion of your limits provokes an argument, greater anger in return, or a lot of denial that they are doing anything, the chances are good that some kind of hurt is intended, even if the other person isn't aware of it.

One of the most effective ways to respond to a passive-aggressive attack is to pick one simple sentence and keep repeating it, without getting drawn into a complicated argument. Or, if you feel you're being treated badly, you might find that the best way to handle the situation is to physically remove yourself, rather than get involved in an argument that you probably aren't going to win. Saying "I don't like this," or "Stop," *and leaving* may ultimately make you feel more powerful, because it deprives the other person of the satisfaction of "getting to you" and gives you the satisfaction of remembering that you can always go somewhere else where you're being treated better.

When Anger Becomes Abuse

Certain types of behavior go beyond "aggression" and "anger" and fall into the category of *abuse*. Abuse is a type of behavior in which one person mistreats another. Abuse may be physical, emotional, or sexual:

- Physical abuse includes hitting, slapping, whipping, hitting someone with an object like an extension cord or a frying pan, throwing objects at someone, pushing or shoving, burning, cutting, and any other kind of physical violence. It doesn't matter whether this sort of abuse is called "punishment"; if it causes physical pain, it's abuse.
- Emotional abuse includes insulting, belittling, continually criticizing, constantly teasing, embarrassing someone, making frightening threats, and devising complicated punishments.
- Sexual abuse includes any kind of sexual contact between an adult and a child or teenager, as well as talking "dirty" or asking someone to talk "dirty"; being naked or partially dressed in front of a child of the opposite sex or watching an opposite-sex child dress, undress, use the toilet, or bathe; caressing, tickling, or playing games that involve a lot of touching; or otherwise invading a child's or teenager's physical privacy. Sexual abuse can be committed by women as well as by men, and it can take place between same-sex as well as opposite-sex people. It's possible that an adult who has no homosexual relationships with other adults will sexually abuse a child of the same sex.

Responding to Abuse

If you are experiencing any of these types of abuse—or if you think you might be—we urge you to get help immediately. If you know anyone who is experiencing these types of abuse, we urge you to help that person get help. An abused person may, like Valerie, worry about what will happen to his or her family if the abuse is discovered, and it's true that reporting abuse might lead to a difficult situation. Nevertheless, if you are being abused, you deserve to get help, so that at the very least you can cope with the effects of being treated that way.

If you are being abused, the best thing you can do for yourself is to find someone to talk to about it, preferably a grown-up. If the person abusing you is not one of your parents, your parents are probably the first people you should tell. Generally, they have the most power to protect you from the abuse of others. If your parents are the abusers, or if you just don't feel comfortable talking to them about being abused, try another adult relative, a teacher, a counselor, a family friend, or a priest, minister, rabbi, or other religious leader. You might also call one of the numbers listed in Chapter 7 of this book; look under "Abuse" or "Social Services" in your local Yellow Pages; or call a hot line and ask for referrals (other places to call). It may take you a while to find someone who believes you, or someone who is willing to help. Don't give up. If the first person you talk to isn't helpful, try someone else—and keep trying until you get the help you need.

You should be aware that telling someone about being abused may have consequences. Certain adults—like teachers and doctors—are often required by law to report suspected physical or sexual abuse. Telling some people about abuse may cause someone to be arrested. It may lead to your and/or your brothers and sisters being taken out of your home, temporarily or permanently. It may also cause other family members to become angry with you, for a short or even a long time.

Deciding whether to tell about physical or sexual abuse may not be an easy decision—but we believe it's almost always the best decision. No matter what mixture of good or bad consequences result, we think that in the end, standing up for yourself and your right not to be abused is the most important thing.

If you're not ready to deal with all the consequences of reporting physical or sexual abuse, you might find a hot line or some other kind of counseling that allows you to keep your identity confidential. And of course, it may also be helpful to tell a trusted friend. It's important to have someone to talk to who understands that the abuse is *not your fault*, and that you have the right to set limits and to live without abuse.

If you're the target of someone else's emotional abuse, your situation is a little more complicated. It's very difficult to define emotional abuse legally, and in many places it is not against the law; or if it is, there are only vague enforcement mechanisms to deal with it. Nevertheless, it's important for people who are being emotionally abused to get the support and help they need to recognize that the abuse is *not their fault*, and that they, too, have the right to set limits and to live without abuse. People who believe they are being emotionally abused can turn to the same places for help as targets of other types of abuse, even if the consequences may be different. (For more suggestions on coping with another person's anger or abuse, see Chapter 6. You might also look at *Straight Talk About Child Abuse*, by Susan Mufson, C.S.W., and Rachel Kranz.)

Getting Help

Whether you're the target of someone's abuse or simply the target of someone's anger, you may find that you need help handling the pain, frustration, and sense of inadequacy that might result. You may also decide that you need help in setting limits, in asserting yourself, or in discovering new ways to handle angry situations.

People often find that one of the most undermining effects of being the target of someone else's anger is their own sense that they are as "bad"—as worthless, undeserving, or misbehaving—as the angry person says they are. But *we* say that, no matter how you've behaved, you have the right to be treated with dignity, honesty, and respect. If you have trouble believing that, we hope you'll turn to Chapters 6 and 7 for ideas on how to find someone who will help you believe in your rights and your worth—someone who will be on your side.

6

Getting Help

Theo finds out about a group that he thinks might help his friend Laurence. It's called Al-a-Teen, and it's a place where teenagers who know someone with a drinking problem can go. An Al-a-Teen group meets at their local "Y." Laurence wants to go, but he's scared. He asks Theo to go with him, and although Theo is scared, too, he wants to help his friend, so he agrees.

The Al-a-Teen meeting is actually very interesting. Most of the time is taken up by teenagers talking about their own experiences with parents, relatives, or friends who have drinking problems. Some of the speakers just tell stories. Others tell what they've been learning: "I can't control another person's drinking; I can only control my own actions," or "It's still so painful, but I just try to take it one day at a time." Afterward, Laurence tells Theo that it made him feel better just to sit in the same room and know that so many other people had the same problem that he did.

Mary Ellen feels better now that she's talking to Lissa, but she's still having more headaches than she would like. The doctor says they're just "stress" and refuses to give her any medication for them. Lissa suggests that Mary Ellen go talk to the school counselor about the things that are bothering her.

"Oh, I couldn't," says Mary Ellen.

"You talk to me," says Lissa.

"But you're my best friend. I couldn't say these things to a stranger."

"Actually, it's easier sometimes talking to a stranger," Lissa says. "They have a different perspective. And you know you're never going to see them except when you're talking to them—it's not like they're going to turn up at your birthday party or something. So you really can tell them things that you don't want even your friends to know. Besides, they're trained in helping people. What do *I* know?"

Mary Ellen worries that if she goes to talk to the school counselor about her problems, it's like she's admitting that she's really screwed up. But Lissa says, "Well, actually, I've talked to her sometimes, when something gets too much for me."

Mary Ellen really admires Lissa—she certainly doesn't think Lissa is messed up! "Maybe I will talk to the counselor," she thinks. "I could at least give it a try."

As Scott and Julia feared, Valerie's situation is getting worse. Although her mother's beatings haven't increased, Valerie is finding that she's losing self-confidence, she can't concentrate on her schoolwork, and she just doesn't feel like doing anything any more. She doesn't want to get her mother in trouble—but she does want to talk to someone about her problem.

At first, Valerie calls a hot line that she sees advertised on a city bus. She knows that no one on the other end of the phone will have any idea who she is, so she can talk about her problem without worrying about what will happen to anyone else besides her. The counselors on the hot line are sympathetic, and mostly they just listen, but every so often, someone does ask Valerie if she'd like to get more help.

Finally, Valerie calls a social-service agency number they give her. The next thing she knows, a social worker comes to the house and talks to Valerie's mother. Valerie isn't sure what will happen next—but she realizes that she feels relieved. Finally, her terrible secret seems to be out in the open. At least now somebody besides her, Scott, and Julia knows what's going on. Even if her mother's behavior doesn't change, Valerie is no longer alone in dealing with it.

Tina and her father have been fighting even more than usual lately. Tina tries to stay focused on what she wants and not get drawn into a battle, but sometimes she forgets. She gets angry, and she finds herself yelling at her father. Or he starts yelling at her—and she just can't keep from shouting back. Finally, Tina's mother says she's had enough. She's made an appointment with a family counselor for everybody in the family. "This is something we all need to work out," she says. "It's not good for any of us to have all this fighting all the time."

At their first session, the family counselor meets everybody—Tina's mother, her father, Tina, and Tina's older sister Lorna. They all sit down together in the counselor's office and take turns explaining what they think the problem is. The counselor doesn't talk much, but she asks a lot of questions, and she makes sure that everybody gets to say what's on his or her mind. Tina can't quite tell why, but even after the first meeting, when nothing much gets decided, she feels a little bit better. Maybe it's just knowing that someone is going to help.

When You Can't Deal with Your Anger by Yourself

There are some problems that you can solve by yourself. But with others, you may need help. If your anger—buried or expressed—is getting in the way of your relationships, your schoolwork, your family time, or your ability to enjoy your life, you might need help in understanding it, dealing with it, expressing it, and letting it go.

If you are experiencing any of the following problems, you should definitely get help. These are not problems that go away by themselves; they are problems that everybody needs help to overcome:

- a problem with drugs or alcohol
- a problem with food—eating compulsively, refusing to eat (anorexia), or eating and purging (using laxatives or vomiting) (bulimia)
- expressing your anger through hitting or other physical violence—or feeling like you might soon do that
- hurting yourself—burning yourself with cigarettes, cutting yourself, or causing yourself physical pain in other ways
- being so angry that you're unable to concentrate
- feeling depressed and hopeless a lot of the time
- crying frequently, either because life seems so upsetting, or for a lot of reasons that don't seem very important
- thoughts about suicide

Asking for Help

As we've said, most people have trouble with anger at some time in their lives. Many people, however, feel uncomfortable about asking for or receiving help. Just the thought of needing or seeking help may bring up one or more of the following feelings:

- **anger**—"Why should I have to ask someone else to help me? I'm good enough to handle this on my own!"
- **shame**—"If I need help, there must be something really wrong with me."
- **fear**—"If I tell someone the truth about how I'm feeling or about what's going on with me, what will they do to me? *Someone* is sure to punish me!"

- **guilt**—"My parents are supposed to be helping me. If I ask someone else for help, it will bring shame on the family."
- **hopelessness**—"Probably no one can help me anyway."
- **anxiety**—"What if I ask for help and it turns out that no one can help me?"
- **sadness**—"When I think about getting help, I think about this problem, and that just makes me so sad."

Of course, people also experience positive feelings at the idea of finding help, feelings such as the following:

- **hope**—"Maybe someone can help me, and my life really can get better."
- **relief**—"I've been trying to fix this on my own, and I just can't. Maybe someone else can show me how."
- **excitement**—"Wouldn't it be great not to have this old problem any more!"

Usually, people feel a mixture of emotions about getting help—sometimes positive, sometimes negative, sometimes both at once or switching back and forth. If you've decided you want help dealing with your anger—or with someone else's anger—*don't give up!* You may find help easily, or you might have to put some effort into it; you may get help from the first place you try, or you might have to keep looking until you find the help that is right for you. But help for you is out there, and you deserve to have all the resources you need in making your life be the way you want it.

What Kinds of Help You Might Find

What kinds of help are available for dealing with anger? Here are a few suggestions (for more specific ideas on getting help, see Chapter 7):

Counseling

An individual counselor will talk to you about your feelings, help you to see problems from a new angle, and point out options that you might not have thought of. Some counselors focus on giving advice or helping with short-term problems. Others focus on helping you understand your feelings, working with you over several months or years. You might find a counselor at your school, at a social service agency or community center, at your church or synagogue, or through your family doctor. You might also find out about counselors through some of the organizations listed in Chapter 7. If you feel you want to talk to a counselor and you don't know how to find one, you might ask a grown-up you trust, call a hot line of any kind and explain what you're looking for, or look in the Yellow Pages under *psychotherapy*.

Family Counseling

A family counselor is just like an individual counselor, except that he or she also talks to families as a group. That's because problems frequently affect more than one family member. It's very rare that only one person in a family has a problem—in fact, some people would say that it's impossible. If you are disturbed by something, chances are there is something troubling other members of your family, too, even if it doesn't look that way. A family counselor helps people understand how they are affecting their fellow family members and suggests options for working out problems that people in the family might not see by themselves. You can usually find family counselors the same way you find other counselors (see the previous paragraph). If your parents are reluctant to see a counselor, it might help to ask another sympathetic adult or relative to talk to them about it. Or you might be able to see the family counselor by yourself in order to discuss ways of encouraging the rest of your family to join you.

Al-a-Teen, Nar-a-Teen, and Other Self-Help Programs

Self-help groups like Alcoholics Anonymous were founded so that people with drinking problems could help themselves and each other to stop drinking and reshape their lives. Then the families of people with substance abuse problems realized that they, too, needed help. Al-Anon was founded for people who were close to someone with a drinking problem, so that they could discuss their anger, their frustration, and their grief. They could also help each other learn to let go and allow their loved ones to work out their problems by themselves. Al-a-Teen works on the same principle, except that it's explicitly for teenagers. It's a place to go if you are close to someone with a drinking problem. Nar-a-Teen is for teenagers who are close to someone with a drug problem. (See Chapter 7 for phone numbers and addresses.)

Support groups

Your school, community center, church, or synagogue may have a support group for young people. A support group is a place where people get together and talk about what's bothering them. Frequently, they offer each other suggestions and insights about what's going on. Usually, support groups for young people include an adult leader who can help make sure that discussion goes smoothly and productively. People in support groups say that just knowing that they're not the only ones going through a problem helps to lighten the burden.

What You Can Expect from a Counselor

At your first meeting with a counselor, he or she may ask you several questions, trying to get basic information about your life. Or you may have already given information to another person at the counselor's office or agency. Some counselors prefer not to gather information at the beginning, but to let whatever they need to know emerge gradually from the counseling sessions.

Most counseling sessions last from 45 to 50 minutes and take place at least once a week. After the first session, most sessions will consist of your talking about whatever is on your mind, with your counselor occasionally asking questions, making suggestions, or offering comments.

A counselor's job is to help you figure out options that you might not have thought of—ways of seeing a problem and handling a situation that might not have occurred to you by yourself. A counselor's job is also to help you become comfortable with all of your feelings—even the feelings that you may feel bad, guilty, or ashamed about. Many counselors give special attention to helping people feel comfortable with their anger, since they know that in our society, anger is an especially troubling emotion for many people.

Most counselors listen more than they talk. They ask questions more than they offer advice. They may make suggestions, but they are there to respond to you, so if something they say makes you uncomfortable or uncertain, they'll expect to talk about your reactions with you.

Family counselors help people in families talk to each other more openly and honestly. They too suggest ways of looking at a problem or handling a situation that family members might not have thought of. Often, the family counselor's role is to make sure that every family member can really hear and understand the points of view of all the other members of the family.

The important thing to remember when working with a counselor is that in the end, making changes in your life is up to you. If you feel that a counselor is on your side, is helpful, and understands what you're saying, then you're probably getting the help you need. If you have a bad feeling about your counselor, you might need to discuss it with him or her—or you might need to consider finding someone else to go to for help. Of course, there are conflicts and problems in relationships with counselors, as in all human relationships. Sometimes, you'll almost certainly be mad at something your counselor says or doesn't say. If your counselor is someone you trust, however, you can work out the problems you have with him or her. In fact, working out conflicts with your counselor is probably the best practice for working out conflicts with other people elsewhere in your life.

Anger's Place in Your Life

As we've seen throughout this book, understanding and dealing with anger is often difficult. What's the difference between an understandable outburst and an abusive tantrum? How can you tell whether an action is aggressive or assertive, polite or passive-aggressive, self-protective or unforgiving? How can you come to terms with an emotion that often seems to be telling you that something is wrong—in your world, in your family, in yourself? How can you learn to be comfortable with your own anger when so many people around you are so uncomfortable—with your anger as well as their own?

These are questions that you'll be dealing with for the rest of your life. The answers that work for you now might change by the time you're 20, or 30, or 40—or even by next year! The ways of coping with anger that work inside your family may not work with your friends, or your teachers, or your boss; the new ways of expressing anger that you learn outside your home may not go over so well with family members. Learning how to sort through all the different results and reactions, how to read your own responses, and how to make choices you can live with is really a lifelong process. The good news is that it can be a very rewarding process, a journey of self-discovery, a continual personal

growth. Learning about your own anger is one very important part of your lifelong journey toward becoming the
person you want to be.

7

Where to Find Help

Anger

Many of the organizations listed here can provide referrals or counseling to teenagers in trouble.

Alabama

Contact Mobile
P.O. Box 66608
Mobile, AL 36660-1608
crisis phone: 205-431-5111
business phone: 205-431-4189
available 24 hours a day

Alaska

Alaska Crisis Line
P.O. Box 24098
Anchorage, AK 99524-0985

crisis phone: 907-276-1600 or 800-478-1600
available 24 hours a day

Arizona

Help On Call Crisis Line
P.O. Box 43696
Tucson, AZ 85733
crisis phone: 602-323-9373
business phone: 602-881-8045
available 24 hours a day

Arkansas

Northwest Arkansas Crisis Intervention Center
P.O. Box 1618
Springdale, AR 72765
crisis phone: 501-756-2337
800-640-2680
business phone: 501-756-1995
available 24 hours a day

California

Teen Line
Thalians Mental Health Center
P.O. Box 48750
Los Angeles, CA 90048
statewide toll free: 800-852-8336
crisis phone: 310-855-4673
business phone: 310-855-3401
staffed 6:00 P.M. to 10:00 P.M.

Colorado

Crisis Control
2459 South Ash
Denver, CO 80222
crisis phone: 303-757-0988

303-789-3073
business phone: 303-756-8485
available 24 hours a day

Connecticut

The Samaritans, Inc. of the Capital Region
P.O. Box 12004
Hartford, CT 06112
crisis phone: 203-232-2121
business phone: 203-232-9559
available 24 hours a day

Delaware

Contact Delaware, Inc.
P.O. Box 9525
Wilmington, DE 19805
crisis phone: 302-575-1112
TTY: 302-656-6660
in Delaware: 800-262-9800
business phone: 302-761-9800
available 24 hours a day

District of Columbia

Samaritans of Washington, Inc.
P.O. Box 9814
Washington, DC 20016
crisis phone: 202-362-8100
business phone: 202-362-8858
available 24 hours a day

Florida

Switchboard of Miami, Inc.
75 Southwest 8th Street
Miami, FL 33130
crisis phone: 305-358-4357

The Link (youth hot line): 305-377-8336
business phone: 305-358-1640
available 24 hours a day

Georgia

Emergency Mental Health Service
Fulton County Health Department
99 Butler Street Southeast
Atlanta, GA 30303
crisis phone: 404-730-1600
TTY: 404-730-1611
business phone: 404-730-1600
available 24 hours a day

Hawaii

Volunteer Information and Referral Service
680 Iwilei Road
#430
Honolulu, HI 96817
Suicide and Crisis Center: 808-521-4555
crisis phone: 808-521-4556
business phone: 808-536-7234
available 24 hours a day

Idaho

Emergency Line
Region IV Service/Mental Health Center
4355 Emerald
Boise, ID 83706
crisis phone: 208-334-0808
business phone: 208-334-0800
available 24 hours a day

Illinois

Affiliated Psychologist Ltd.
4801 West Peterson
Suite 525
Chicago, IL 60646
crisis phone: 312-286-3100
business phone: 312-286-3100
available 24 hours a day

Indiana

Mental Health Association in Marion County
Crisis and Suicide Intervention Service
2506 Willowbrook Parkway
#100
Indianapolis, IN 46205-1542
crisis phone: 317-251-7575
business phone: 317-251-0005
available 24 hours a day

Iowa

Community Telephone Service Crisis Line
Service of the American Red Cross
2116 Grand Avenue
Des Moines, IA 50312
crisis phone: 515-244-1000
counseling: 515-244-1010
AIDS Hotline Statewide: 800-445-2437
business phone: 515-244- 6700
available Monday–Thursday 3:00 P.M. to 8:00 A.M.
Friday–Sunday 24 hours

Kansas

Wyandotte Mental Health Center/County Crisis Line
36th and Eaton
Kansas City, KS 66103

crisis phone: 913-831-1773
business phone: 913-831-9500
available 24 hours a day

Kentucky

The Crisis and Information Center
137 West Muhammad Ali Boulevard
Louisville, KY 40202-1429
crisis phone: 502-589-4313
TDD: 502-589-4259
Kentucky Watts Line: 800-221-0446
FAX: 502-589-8756
business phone: 502-589-8615 Extension 420
available 24 hours a day

Louisiana

Volunteer and Information Agency
4747 Earhart Boulevard
Suite 111
New Orleans, LA 70125
crisis phone: 504-523-2673
business phone: 504-488-4636
available 24 hours a day

Maine

Crisis Stabilization Unit
P.O. Box 588
Skowhegan, ME 04976
crisis phone: 207-474-2506
Skowhegan (Dispatcher): 800-452-1933
children's services only: 800-400-2564
business phone: 207-474-2564
available 24 hours a day

Maryland

First Step Youth Services Center
8303 Liberty Road
Baltimore, MD 21207
crisis phone: 410-521-3800
business phone: 410-521-4141
available Monday to Thursday 9:00 A.M. to 9:00 P.M.;
Friday 9:00 A.M. to 5:00 P.M.

Massachusetts

The Samaritans
500 Commonwealth Avenue
Boston, MA 02215
crisis phone: 617-247-0220
Samariteen Line, 3:00-9:00 P.M. daily: 617-247-8050
toll free, MA & NH only: 800-252-8336
business phone: 617-536-2460
available 24 hours a day
walk-in 8:00 A.M. to 8:00 P.M. daily

Michigan

NSO Emergency Telephone Service/
  Suicide Prevention Center
220 Bagley
Suite 626
Detroit, MI 48226
crisis phone: 313-224-7000
business phone: 313-961-1060
available 24 hours a day

Minnesota

Crisis Intervention Center
Hennepin County Medical Center
701 Park Avenue South
Minneapolis, MN 55415

crisis connection line: 612-379-6363
suicide line: 612-347-2222
crisis home program: 612-347-3170
sexual assault line: 612-347- 5838
Behavioral Emergency Outreach: 612-347-2011
business phone: 612-347-3164
available 24 hours a day

Mississippi

Contact Helpline
P.O. Box 1304
Columbus, MS 39703
crisis phone: 601-328-0200
601-327-4357
business phone: 601-327-2968

Missouri

Life Crisis Services, Inc.
1423 South Big Bend Boulevard
St. Louis, MO 63117
adults: 314-647-4357
teens: 314-644-5886
business phone: 314-647-3100
available 24 hours a day

Montana

Billings Helpline
Yellowstone Mental Health Association
1245 North 29th Avenue
Billings, MT 59191
crisis phone: 406-252-1212
business phone: 406-657-3120
available 24 hours a day

Nebraska

Father Flanagan's Boys' Home
Boys Town National Hotline
Town Hall
Boys Town, NE 68010
national hotline: 800-448-3000
 national hotline TDD: 800-448- 1833
 available 24 hours a day

Nevada

State of Nevada Mental Heath
Division of Child and Family Services
6171 West Charleston
Las Vegas, NV 89158
702-486-6100

New Hampshire

Mental Health Center of Greater Manchester
401 Cypress Street
Manchester, NH 03103
603-668-4111
available 24 hours a day

New Jersey

Emergency Psychiatric Services
100 Bergen Street
Newark, NJ 07103
main number: 201-623-2323
business phone: 201-982-4818
available 24 hours a day

New Mexico

Crisis Unit
Bernalillo Mental Health Center

2600 Marble Northeast
Albuquerque, NM 87106
505-843-2800
available 24 hours a day

New York

The Samaritans of New York City
P.O. Box 1259
Madison Square Station
New York, NY 10159
crisis phone: 212-673-3000
business phone: 212-677-3009
available 24 hours a day

North Carolina

Contact: Winston-Salem
1111 West First Street
Winston-Salem, NC 27101
crisis phone: 910-722-5153
teenline, 3:00-7:00 P.M. weekdays: 910-723-8336
business phone: 910-723-4338
available 24 hours a day

North Dakota

Help-Line
c/o Mental Health Association of North Dakota
P.O. Box 160
Bismarck, ND 58502
crisis phone: 800-472-2911
business phone: 701-255-3692
available 24 hours a day

Ohio

St. Vincent Charity Hospital
Psychiatric Emergency Service

2351 East 22nd Street
Cleveland, OH 44115
crisis phone: 216-229-2211
business phone: 216-861-6200
available 24 hours a day

Oklahoma

Teenline, Oklahoma City
Department of Mental Health
P.O. Box 53277
Oklahoma City, OK 73152
local: 405-271-8336
statewide toll free: 800-522-8336
business phone: 405-271-8755
available noon-midnight

Oregon

Metro Crisis Intervention Service
P.O. Box 637
Portland, OR 97207
crisis phone: 503-223-6161
business phone: 503-226-3099
available 24 hours a day

Pennsylvania

Philadelphia Suicide and Crisis Center
1 Reading Center
1101 Market, 7th Floor
Philadelphia, PA 19107
crisis phone: 215-686-4420
business phone: 215-592-5565
available 24 hours a day

Rhode Island

The Samaritans of Rhode Island
2 Magee Street
Providence, RI 02906
crisis phone: 401-272-4044
Rhode Island only: 800-365-4044
business phone: 401-272-4243
available 24 hours a day

South Carolina

Hotline
P.O. Box 71583
North Charleston, SC 29415-1583
crisis phone: 803-744-4357
statewide: 800-922-2283
teenline 4:00 to 8:00 P.M. Monday–Friday: 803-747-8336
teenline 4:00 to 8:00 P.M. Monday–Friday: 800-273-8225
business phone: 803-747-3007
available 24 hours a day

South Dakota

Crisis Line, Volunteer and Information Center
Family Services
3011 S. Phillips Avenue
Sioux Falls, SD 57105
crisis phone: 605-339-4357
business phone: 605-334-6646
available 24 hours a day

Tennessee

Charter Lakeside Hospital
2911 Brunswick Road
Memphis, TN 38133
crisis phone: 800-232-5253
  800-443-6464

901-377-4733
business phone: 901-377-4700
available 24 hours a day

Texas

Contact 214
P.O. Box 800742
Dallas, TX 75380-0742
crisis phone: 214-233-2233
teen contact: 214-233-8336
business phone: 214-233-0866
available 24 hours a day

Utah

Logan Helpline
121 A UMC
Utah State University
Logan, UT 84322
crisis phone: 801-752-3964
Utah only: 800-626-8399
business phone: 801-797-1647

Vermont

Hotline For Help, Inc.
17 Elliot Street
Brattleboro, VT 05301
crisis phone: 802-257-7989
available to ME, NH, & VT: 800-257-7980
business phone: 802-257-7980
available 24 hours a day

Washington

Crisis Clinic of King County
1515 Dexter Avenue North
#300

Seattle, WA 98109
crisis phone: 206-461-3222
business phone: 206-461-3210
available 24 hours a day

West Virginia

Upper Ohio Valley Crisis Helpline
P.O. Box 653
Wheeling, WV 26003
crisis phone: 304-234-8161
business phone: 304-234-1848
available 24 hours a day

Wisconsin

Helpline
2266 North Prospect Avenue
Suite 324
Milwaukee, WI 53202
crisis phone: 414-271-3123
TDD: 414-271-6039
business phone: 414-276-8487
available 24 hours a day

Wyoming

Cheyenne Helpline
P.O. Box 404
Cheyenne, WY 82001
307-634-4469
available 24 hours a day

Canada

Distress Centre of Ottawa
P.O. Box 70039
160 Elgin Street Main Plaza
Ottawa, ON K2P 2M3

crisis phone: 613-238-3311
youthline (peer staffed): 613-238-2088
Deep River line: 800-267-7799
drug helpline: 800-567-3784
business phone: 613-238-1089
available 9:00 A.M. to 5:00 P.M. Monday–Friday

Toronto East General Hospital
Department of Psychiatry
825 Coxwell Avenue
Toronto, ON M4C 3E7
business phone: 416-461-8272
crisis phone: 416-461-0311, 9-5 (Mon–Fri.)
  (recording after hours)

Saskatoon Crisis Intervention Service
1410 20th Street West
Saskatoon, SK S7M 0Z4
306-933-6077
available 24 hours a day

Additional Resources

The following organizations can provide you with referrals and advice in dealing with problems that may be related to teenage anger.

Alcohol and Drug Problems

Al-Anon Family Group Headquarters
1372 Broadway
New York, NY 10018
212-302-7240
See the white pages for the group in your area. Al-Anon
  helps those over the age of 13 deal with alcohol problems
  in their families.

Al-a-Teen
P.O. Box 862
Midtown Station
New York, NY 10018-0862
212-302-7240
This organization helps teenagers whose lives have been affected by another person's alcoholism.

Alcoholics Anonymous and World Services
475 Riverside Drive, 11th Floor
New York, NY 10115
212-870-3400
This organization provides free referrals for those seeking recovery from alcohol problems.

Nar-a-Teen
c/o Nar-Anon Family Group Headquarters, Inc.
P.O. Box 2562
Palos Verdes Peninsula, CA 90274
310-547-5800
This organization helps teenagers whose lives have been affected by another person's drug abuse.

Narcotics Anonymous and World Services Office
P.O. Box 9999
Van Nuys, CA 91409
818-780-3951
This organization provides general reference services for those seeking recovery from narcotics addiction.

Eating Disorders

Adolescent Clinic
Toronto Hospital for Sick Children
555 University Avenue
7th Floor
Toronto, Ontario
Canada M5G 1X8
416-813-5804

American Anorexia/Bulimia Association, Inc. (AA/BA)
  418 E. 76 St.
  NY, NY 10021
  212-891-8686

Anorexia Nervosa and Related Eating Disorders, Inc.
  (ANRED)
  P.O. Box 5102
  Eugene, OR 97405
  503-344-1144

Youth Clinic
Children's Hospital of Vancouver
401 North Esmond
Burnaby, British Columbia
Canada V5C 1S4
604-291-6786

Physical and Sexual Abuse

American Humane Association
63 Inverness Drive East
Englewood, CO 80112
303-792-9900

Children's Aid Society
33 Charles Street East
Toronto, Ontario
Canada M4Y 1R9
416-924-4646

National Committee for Prevention of Child Abuse
332 South Michigan Avenue
Suite 1600
Chicago, IL 60604
312-663-3520

For Further Reading

The following books will provide further information on anger.

Amos, Jeanine. *Angry*. New York: Steck Vaughn Publishers, 1991.

Ellis, Albert. *Anger: How to Live With and Without It*. Flushing, N.Y.: Asia Book Corporation of America, 1987.

Freeman, Lucy. *Our Inner World of Rage: Understanding and Transforming the Power of Anger*. New York: Crossroad Publishing Co., 1991.

Gelinas, Paul J. *Coping with Anger*. New York: Rosen Publishing Co., 1988.

Hankins, Gary. *Prescription for Anger: Coping with Angry Feelings and Angry People*. New York: Warner Books, Inc., 1993.

McKay, Matthew. *When Anger Hurts*. New York: Fine Communications Co., 1994.

Riley, Sue. *Angry*. New York: Children's Publishing Co., 1988.

Rubin, Theodore Isaac. *The Angry Book*. New York: New American Library, 1973.

Tavris, Carol. *Anger: The Misunderstood Emotion*. New York: Simon & Schuster, 1989.

Williams, Redford. *Anger Kills: How to Control the Hostility That Can Harm Your Health*. New York: Random House, Inc., 1993.

INDEX